COSTUME OF
HOUSEHOLD SERVANTS

Upper. COACHMAN Livery overcoat and suit. Outmoded tricorne hat, wig, breeches and buckled shoes as worn in the eighteenth century.

Lower left. HOUSEKEEPER wearing typical chatelaine and working apron.

Lower centre. BUTLER in tailcoat and elaborately frilled shirt but old fashioned in wearing breeches and wig.

Lower right. LADY'S MAID in the typical wide-shouldered, wide-hatted elegance of her period. Her apron is decorative rather than functional.

Drawn and engraved by R. Cruikshank 1827, coloured impression, author's collection.

Costume of
HOUSEHOLD SERVANTS

*From the Middle Ages
to 1900*

Phillis Cunnington

ADAM AND CHARLES BLACK
LONDON

First published 1974

A. & C. Black Limited

4, 5 & 6 Soho Square, London W1V 6AD

© 1974 Phillis Cunnington

ISBN 0 7136 1393 9

Photoset by Filmtype Services Limited
and printed in Great Britain by
BAS Printers Limited, Wallop, Hampshire

Contents

Plates

Acknowledgements

I should like to thank the following for expert help: Mrs M. Boston, Dr F. G. Emmison, Mr J. Hull, Kent County Archivist, Major and Mrs Mansfield, Mr G. H. Stott (photographer) and Mr A. A. Whife of the *Tailor and cutter*.

I also wish to thank the Staffs of the following institutions: British Museum (Department of Printed Books, of MSS, and of Prints and Drawings), Strangers' Hall Museum, Norwich, Courtauld Institute of Art, The Guildhall Library, the University of London Library, York Public Library, the Gallery of English Costume, Manchester, the Costume Galleries, Castle Howard, York. I am specially grateful to Mr F. C. Morgan and his daughter of Hereford Cathedral Library, for valuable help with some illustrations. My gratitude is also due to my daughter Mrs Luckham for very valuable help throughout. I owe a deep debt of gratitude to Miss Catherine Lucas for her untiring aid in research and for reading my text before publication and making valuable suggestions, and finally to Dr Alexander Walk for a thorough reading of the page proofs which has been the means of saving me from various slips and errors.

PHILLIS CUNNINGTON

CHAPTER ONE

Classification of servants: their titles and occupations

This book describes the costume of English servants through the centuries. It will be helpful to give a list of the various grades of servants employed and their duties, which have some bearing on their costume.

MEDIEVAL AND SIXTEENTH CENTURY

The number serving one master or mistress varied according to the size of the household. In the Middle Ages the serving man played an important part in the upkeep of his master's estate, and each servant had his specific task to perform. A list of some of the more important men servants is found in the *Boke of Curtasye, c.* 1430–40 (in *The Babees Book* p. 309 seq.)*.

1. *The Steward* was the head servant. He had to superintend the management of the whole household. We find this statement in Spenser's *Faerie Queen* 1590:

> The first of them that eldest was and best
> Of all the house, had charge and government
> As Guardian and *Steward* of the rest.

2. *The Marshal* "an officer charged with the duty of regulating processions and ceremonies, deciding on points of precedence and maintaining order".
3. *The Chamberlain* was in charge of his master's apartments and might even act as his valet.
4. *The Gentleman Usher*, a servant in charge of the door and whose business it was to introduce guests and see that all above stairs "are civil". The duty of the Gentleman Usher was

---

* For full specifications of books referred to, see Bibliography.

1

to govern all above stairs or in the presence of his lord . . . to see the greate chamber bee fynne and neatlie kepte . . . and to have at commaundemente all the gentlemen and yeomen wayters and to see into their behaviours and fashion, that they be civill . . . and if any defecte bee, in any of them, they are to instruct them in courteous manner which is both good for them, and bettereth the lord's service.

5. *The Page*, a boy of gentle birth who gave his services in exchange for an aristocratic upbringing. His clothes were provided.
6. *The Herald*, an important person sent to deliver messages for his master, and act as master of ceremonies, e.g. at tournaments.
7. *The Panter* or Pantler, later butler, was in charge of the pantry and the distribution of bread.

And if thou be admitted in any offyce as Butler or Panter – in some places they are both one . . . in your offyce of the Pantrye see that your bread be chipped and squared . . . and see your napry be cleane.

Book of Nurture, *c.* 1465, *Babees Book*, p. 66

The term *panter* came to an end in the 16th century although still used by Shakespeare in *King Henry IV*, Part 2, V, iv, 258–61 :

Falstaff: A good shallow young fellow
A' would have made a good Pantler
A' would have chipped bread well.   1597–8

8. *The Gentleman-in-Waiting*, later called the *Valet*. All the upper class servants were usually "persons of gentle blood and slender fortune" and they dressed in the fashion of their day.

There were other upper class servants. *The Clerk of the Kitchen* had to serve the meals from the kitchen. He also had to keep account of purchases and sometimes preside at table. A Squire was master of the horse and under him the Avener was in charge of the stables. The Squire, however, might have other duties when belonging to a royal household and was then known as Squire for the body, meaning a valet (q.v.).

Royal Household servants had special duties. *The Squire of the Body* [valet] fifteenth century, at the Court of Henry VII was important.

Item, the squyeres for the body they ought to array the Kinge; and to vnaray hym and no man els to sett hand vpon the Kinge; and the yoman or grome of the robes to take vnto thre squyeres for ye body all the King's stuf as well he shone as his oyr [other] gere . . . and at the King's vprissinge . . . the vscher muste se that the wache be sett ready for the King's ablusions.

Antiquarian Repertory, Vol. I, ed. F. Grose, p. 306

The King's Chamberlain also, at a meal, had to have a towel or napkin with which to handle the dishes so as not to touch them and having received them from the hands of the Sewer he had to taste the "spice-dish" to ensure the King's safety.

The Sewer[1] or table attendant. He had to set the table for the King and fetch the King's food from the kitchen. When the King's meal was over, he had to fetch a towel, carry it on his shoulder ready for the King when he washed in the King's chamber, and finally he had to

stand still till the Kerver come; and the Kerver muste se that pantere tak ye assay [i.e. sample] of the bred, salt, and trenchours; then the Kerver to cutt.

Ibid.

The Queen's servants at the court of Henry VII were also important. There was the *Lady Governor of the Nursery*, and the *Dry Nurse*. The ladies were supervised by the Chamberlain and waited on by the King's servants. There was also a *Physician* who watched over the child's nourishment to see that it was properly fed.

Servants involved in the ceremonies of hand-washing before and after meals at Henry VII's court were the King's and the Queen's Carver[2] and Sewer, who had to carry the towels. The usher had to fill the basin with water, then

two Squyeres to . . . tak up the borde [tray] and lay it down afore the Kinge and then the Uschere to knelle down and make clene the King's skirts . . . then the bishop . . . to say grace.

Ibid, p. 296

Again, for Royalty, a list of some of the servants required about the Court of Henry VIII was drawn up at the king's command by the Earl of Arundel, Lord Chamberlain from 1526 to 1530. The list is as follows:

[1] A person charged with the service of the table – a head servant, from the French "asseoir".

[2] From the beginning of the fifteenth century the King's "Carver" held an office unrelated to domestic affairs, e.g. held by Sir John Howard in 1461.

Knights and Esquires of the Body [valets]
Gentleman Usher
Yoman Usher
Sewer of the Chambre
Yoman of the Crowne of the Garde and King's Chamber
Grome Porter
Groome of the King's Chamber, sometimes had to serve at meals.
Page of the King's Chamber

Their duties would be similar to those in the last reign, but some are given in more detail.

First *the page* "who had to rise early, make his own bed and others "to make fyres in every chamber", to put straw on the floors, and do a lot of housework. Also he must be ready at any time "to do messages" i.e. run errands, "or any other services, to my L. Chamberlayn, or any other officers under him". Later the making up of the King's bed was the responsibility of several servants. A *groom* or a *page* by the light of a torch had to collect the bedding from the wardrobe and the bed was then made by a gentleman usher and two or three yomen under his command. One yoman had a dagger with which

> to serche the strawe of the King's bedde, that their be none vntruthe therin. And then thes yomen to cast upon the bed of down vpon that, and oon of them to tumble over it for the serche therof.
>
> *Ibid.*

A Fool was sometimes kept for the purpose of entertainment in a very swell household or by Royalty.

More humble servants. There were waiters, usually called "cup-bearers"; also henchmen who were male attendants, their duties often overlapping with pages. The kitchen staff included cooks, always men, kitchen boys, and the scullions who cleaned pots and pans and worked in the kitchen. Indoor grooms were men with various tasks who took orders from the gentleman usher. Among outdoor grooms was the one who ran beside his master's bridle and was therefore known as a *footman*. He later became the "running footman".

> Mony of hem fote-men ther ben, that rennen by the brydels of ladys shene [bright].
>
> *Boke of Curtasye* (1430–40), *The Babees Book*

4

WOMEN SERVANTS

Women servants also were divided into upper and lower grades and like the men those in the upper class were usually of gentle or noble birth, such as the lady's gentlewoman or waiting woman, later known as the lady's maid, the housekeeper, the wet nurse and other helpers.

In the lower ranks were the chamber maids, the kitchen maids, nursery maids and sometimes dairy maids. Even a woman cup-bearer has been recorded in the fourteenth century.

Generally speaking the women were of less importance than the men whose work had a much wider range. The number of servants employed varied according to the size of the household; an Earl might have many hundreds, but even the humblest had at least one. The following song shows something of what a maid-of-all-work had to do in the early fourteenth century. It is entitled

The Servant Girl's Holiday
I've waited longing for today;
Spindle bobbin and spool away!
In joy and bliss I'm off to play
   Upon this high holiday.

The dirt upon the floor's unswept,
The fireplace isn't cleaned and kept,
I haven't cut the rushes yet
   Upon this high holiday.

The cooking herbs I must fetch in,
And fix my kerchief under my chin
Darling Jack, lend me a pin
   To fix me well this holiday!

Now midday has almost come,
And all my chores are still not done.
I'll clean my shoes till they become
   Bright for a high holiday.

Medieval English Verse,
ed. Brian Stone, Penguin Classics, 1st pub. 1964, 1970

These girls made the ordinary clothes for themselves and the family, as well as preparing the raw material for simpler garments with the "spindle bobbin and spool".

Jervase Markham[1] in 1598 wrote:

> the good days of domestic service for men of breeding have passed. The
> large households have been cut down for economy's sake; the quality of
> the staff has sadly fallen off. A master is now content to employ the untrained
> sons of husbandmen rather than men of gentle birth and social standing.

He implies that this is partly due to the fact that the family has begun to
spend part of the year in town and partly because of the pressure of
yokels wanting the jobs as servants in order to avoid conscription. Also
there was much less "liberality" – glorified perquisites that made the
job fit for gentlemen.

A curious list of what servants noblemen might keep is given in a late
sixteenth century *Book of Precedence* (B.M. MS. Harl. 1440 f. 14) EETS
extra series VIII (italics ours).

> *A Duke* may have a *Treasuror*, a *Chamberlayne*, 4 great *hushers* [gentlemen
> ushers], a *Steward*, a *Comptrouller*, a Master of his house.

> *An Erle* may have a *secretary*, a *Comptrouller*, a *Steward*, 2 great *hushers*, a
> gentill-man for his house.

> *A Baron* may have a *Steward*, a *Clarke of his kitchen*, a *yeoman* of his horse, a
> *Gentleman husher*, and a *Yeoman Husher*, a *grome of his Chamber*, a *Yemon
> husher of his hall*, and his grome, (but no Marshall), a *sewer*, bearer of dishes
> Armed, a Caruer [carver] (but vnmarried), a *foreman*, his cup (²) couered,
> [t]houghe in the presence of his better but no assay taken at any time.

Henchmen continued as such in the sixteenth century. In Shakespeare's *Midsummer Night's Dream*, Oberon says "I do beg a little
changeling boy to be my henchman" (1590–1).

But earlier than this we are told that

> Her Highness [Queen Elizabeth I] hath of late, whereat some doo moche
> marvel, disolved the auncient office of the Henchemen.
>
> A letter to the Earl of Shrewsbury in 1565,
> *Illustrations of British History*, ed. E. Lodge (3 Vols 1791, 3 Vols 1838)

---

[1] *A Health to the Gentlemanly Profession of Serving-Men*, 1598, by I.M., ed. A. V.
Judges (Shakespeare Assoc. Facsimile No: 3, Oxf.U.P. 1931).

[2] Cup of Assay, the small cup with which the assay (trial) of wine, etc., was made.

Henchmen were employed by the Earl of Northumberland daily to wait at table at informal meals.

> My Lordes first Hanneshman to serve as Cupberer to my Lord. My Lordes II [2nd] Hanshman to serve as cupberer to my Lady.
> > Earl of Northumberland's Household Book (1512 to 1525),
> > *Antiquarian Repertory*, Vol. 4 (1807), ed. F. Grose.

Henchmen continued to be employed as general servants right into the nineteenth century.

The Earl of Northumberland's household is fairly representative of the vast number of servants and retainers employed on a large estate. High ranking servants too had menials working under them, but these were only allowed if paid for by their relations. For instance

> Gentilmen in Householde . . .
> ii Carvers for my Lord's Boorde and a Servant
> betwixt theym, both except thai be at their
> friendis fyndyng [that is expenses paid by their own folk].

Lord Northumberland had his own herald and pursuivant, an officer of arms of lesser rank than the herald which by promotion he might become. His head officers were as usual the chamberlain, the steward, the treasurer and controller. Among the lower ranks are listed "Yomen of the Robes" of the seller, the pantry, the buttery, the ewry and also the baker, the brewer, the caterer, the groom and of course the cook. He also employed three minstrels to play "A Taberett, A Luyte and A Rebecc" and five children

> oon for the Wairdrob, one for the Stabyll,
> oone for the Skullery, one for the Bakhous and
> one for the Chariote.

Among the upper women servants were

> Gentillwomen for my Lady – iii
> Chamberer for my Lady ii

and for the nursery two Rockers to rock the cradle "and a Childe to attend in the Nursery".

As stated, this household represents servants required by a rich nobleman in the sixteenth century. "The hoole noumbre of all the seid persons in Houshold is CLXVj". (Op. cit.)

7

B

SEVENTEENTH CENTURY

People of position still had a great many servants. Evelyn's father in 1634 when he was appointed Sheriff of Surrey and Sussex had 116 servants in livery "everyone liveried in greene satin doublets" – *Diary* entry for Nov: 5, 1633. Lady Hoby in 1600 had at least ten men serving in the house as well as women servants (*Diary of Lady Margaret Hoby 1599–1605* ed. D. M. Meads). But by the middle of the century, as a result of aristocratic extravagance, the rise in prices and finally the civil war, many re-adjustments had to be made. The castle soon gave way to the gentleman's country seat and gradually gentlemen ceased to be employed as servants, and by the middle of this century livery was worn only by the lower ranks.

The *Steward* was still an important servant but less likely to be of gentle birth. The *gentleman usher's* duties were sometimes carried out by the butler or the footman, or even the housemaid, in spite of a lower rank and the *clerk of the kitchen's* work began to be undertaken by the housekeeper.

The *trencherman* was a resident servant and according to Dr Johnson, he was a cook. He is mentioned by Shakespeare in *Much Ado About Nothing* (1599–1600) I, i, 51.

> You had musty victual and he hath holp
> to eat it; he is a very valient trencherman.

The Chamberlain apart from being in charge of his master's apartments, might also act as his valet at times.

> What! thinkst
> That the bleak air, thy boisterous *Chamberlain*
> Will put thy Shirt on warm?
> 1607–8, Shakespeare, *Timon of Athens*, IV, iii, 51

Servants in the retinue of Sir Richard Fanshawe following the funeral procession of Phillip IV of Spain were

> Chief Secretary, gentleman of the horse, the steward, 3 pages, the butler, the cook, a groom, a laundress and four Spanish footmen.   1665
> *Memoirs of Ann, Lady Fanshawe, 1600–72*, ed. 1907

The gentlemen of the Privy Chamber in Ordinary wait on the king indoors and out when he is on foot and wait at his table when he eats in Privy Chamber "and bring in his Meat. Every Night two of them lie in the King's Privy Chamber" (Chamberlayne, 1669).

A Fool might still be kept by Royalty or persons of rank for their entertainment (see page 4).

If a man was wealthy, he would now have his own coach which would necessitate a coachman and all the servants connected with the stable, including a running footman. His job was to run in front of the coach and give assistance on bad roads, but even more significant was his mere presence which displayed the importance of the travellers in the coach.

> I will dismount, and by the waggon's wheel
> Trot like a servile footman all day long.
> 1600, Shakespeare, *Titus Andronicus*, V, ii, 54

In middle class and professional households the number of men servants might be about eight, but women, who were comparatively unimportant in Tudor times, were now more freely employed. They were cheaper and easier to manage. In all but wealthy households the cook was now a woman and called the *cook-maid* and working under her, the kitchen maid. Other domestics were the *chamber maid*, one of whose duties was washing "fine linen" and starching "lawns" etc.

> Shee is her Mistresses Shee Secretarie, and keeps the box of her teeth, her haire and her painting [make up] very private. Her industrie is up-stairs, and down-staires . . . and by her drie hand you may know shee is a sore starcher.
> Sir Thomas Overbury, *The Overburian Characters*,
> 1615. The Chamber-Mayde (The Percy Reprints No. XIII), ed. W. S. Paylor

Others included the housemaid with general house work to do, and the superior waiting gentlewoman, later called the lady's maid because she attended to the "lady" her mistress in every respect.

Pepys in 1660 had one general maid whose duties included the household washing. But two years later she was promoted and became "my wife's upper mayde". Her brother was Pepys's man servant and there was also a cook maid, "a pretty willing wench but no good cook".

In small households, where only one male servant was kept, quick changes in dress might have to be made according to the task to be performed. This state of affairs was fairly common and continued into the 19th century.

EIGHTEENTH CENTURY

The following is a list of some of the men servants employed in a large household.

The upper servants indoors were:
the butler, the valet, the groom of the chambers, the cook, the clerk of the kitchen, the confectioner, the baker, and the bailiff. Those working outdoors were: the clerk of the stables and the head gardener.

Servants, in livery, below these, were:
the footman, the under-butler, the porter and the page (no longer a gentleman). The rest were mainly outdoor servants as the coachman, the running footman, the groom, the under coachman and postillion and on large estates, the park keeper and game keeper.[1]

"The postillion was one who rides the near horse of the leaders when four or more horses are used in a carriage or post-chaise or who rides the near horse when one pair only is used and there is no driver on the box." (*Century Dictionary*)

> The Coachman, however, did not drive all six, one of the leaders being always ridden by a postillion.
>
> J. Ashton, *Social Life in the Reign of Queen Anne.* 1882

The postillion was, in fact, the coachman's assistant when driving many horses.

There was at this time a great change in the status of the men servants, who were now mostly drawn from a lower social class than formerly. Even upper servants might be the sons of labourers and artisans. The cook was now among the upper ranks.

In middle class homes the duties required of a *footman* might be varied and extensive. Apart from being a male servant who had to accompany his master or mistress when out walking or attend the carriage, the table, etc., in 1738 Mrs. Purefoy wrote:

> I want a footman to work in the garden, lay the cloth, wait at table and go to cart with Thomas when hee is ordered, or do any other businesse hee is ordered to do, and not too large sized a man that hee may not be too great a load for an horse when he rides. Hee must have a good character; hee only goes to cart now and then.
> Your friend E.P.
>
> *Purefoy Letters,* Vol. I

---

[1] *Life in Georgian England* by E. N. Williams, ed. P. Quennell.

1. Butler in evening dress suit, white stockings and waistcoat, 1843.

Waiting at table continued into the next century.

> The dessert was not carried out till after nine; and at ten, footmen were still running to and fro with trays and coffee cups.   1847
> Charlotte Brontë, *Jane Eyre*, ch. XVII

The duties of a butler are described in a cutting from a newspaper of 1843 preserved in the Guildhall Library, to which Fig. 1 was an illustration.

> The butler . . . was a functionary of great importance; his office was to take care of the wine, and hand the first cup to his master on all state occasions, having previously tasted the same, to assure the nobleman to whom he acted as purveyor, no deleterious compound had entered therein . . . .
>
> Independently of the management of the cellar . . . he has the care of the plate chest . . . which in some families is no inconsiderable trust.

Women servants continued as previously.

A new term was used by Richardson in his *Clarissa Harlowe* 1748. This was a "varletesse" who corresponded to a male valet. She was in fact a lady's maid.

The housekeeper was in charge of the maid servants and she had "to be up in the morning before any of the servants, and let them never go to bed until they have seen the doors and windows properly fastened".

She was also in charge of provisions and had to be "as frugal in the purchase of them as if they were for herself" (Anne Barker, *The Complete Servant Maid c.* 1770).

The lady's maid had charge of her mistress's wardrobe and also had to assist her mistress dressing and sometimes arrange her hair in the correct style. Betsy Sheridan (Sheridan's sister) wrote a letter in 1790 saying how pleased she was to have managed without her maid's assistance when preparing for a ball at Bath.

> I was provident enough never to suffer the Maid I kept to dress me so constantly as to lose the power of arranging my own locks, which by the bye I have so far recovered that I have completely thrown off my wig.
>
> *Betsy Sheridan Journal, 1784–6 and 1788–90,* ed. by William Lefanu

Another task devolving on her was the washing "of laces, muslin, gauzes, cambricks, also to clean gold and silver lace, stuffs, etc." (Anne Barker, *The Complete Servant Maid c.* 1770).

A maid servant in this century might have very varied tasks to perform.

> The Chambermaid's first consideration . . . the case of her mistress's cloaths . . . Let your respective cloaths, either for dress or undress, be always deposited in their different departments.
>
> *Ibid, c.* 1770

For a maid servant to act as footman or body-servant to her master comes as a surprise. However, Steele, writing as Isaac Bickerstaff in the *Tatler* (No. 132) about his club, says:

> This may suffice to give the world a taste of our innocent conversation which we spun out until about ten of the clock, when my *maid* came with a lantern to light me home. 1709

Even as late as 1895 we find a newspaper advertising for

> A good Parlourmaid, aged about 24, tall, no fringe . . . must valet a gentleman.

NINETEENTH CENTURY

The number of servants employed in a large establishment was still great. They usually consisted of a house steward, a butler, a valet and a male or female cook. There might be about six kitchen helpers male and female. There were a number of footmen, an usher in livery, a Victorian innovation since upper servants long since ceased to be thus attired; also a page.

Among women servants there would be the housekeeper, the lady's maid, and a smart, preferably tall, parlourmaid to assist or replace a footman. Housemaids or chambermaids kept the rooms clean and there might be laundry maids and stillroom maids as well.

In households with children there would be the nursery staff, headed by the children's nurse, later known as the nanny, and sometimes there was the French "bonne" in attendance. There might also be a schoolroom staff, perhaps including a French governess and a schoolroom maid. Here is what Samuel and Sarah Adams have to say about "*The Head Nurse*".

> This important servant ought to be of a lively and cheerful disposition . . . clean and neat in her habits and person.
>
> *The Complete Servant*, 1825

If outdoor servants were employed these might include a "tiger". He was "a groom who goes out with the equipage of his master, that is with the dog cart, curricle, cab, or other vehicle driven by his master . . . his duty being to take care of the equipage when the master has left the box". (*Century Dictionary*) He was humorously compared to a tiger in a show-wagon, driven about the streets on parade, hence his name.

The ancient method of hiring the lower grade country servants for smaller households was still practised in the earlier years of the nineteenth century. The girls would appear for hire at the annual mop or fair. A cook would wear a red ribbon and carry a basting ladle, the emblem of her profession, while a housemaid would have a blue ribbon and carry a broom. This custom came to an end by 1865 for house servants, though farm workers sometimes continued thus to present themselves for hire at these fairs.

The number of servants (fictional) kept in 1840 is given in Frances Trollope's *Life and Adventures of Michael Armstrong*:

> Lady Dowling kept two carriages, six horses, one coachman, one postillion, five gardeners, two grooms, three footmen, one butler, and a page – not to mention two nurses, four nursery-maids, and more ladies' maids, housemaids, cookmaids, kitchen-maids, laundry-maids, still-room maids, dairy-maids and the like, than any other lady in the county.

In small middle class households where only one male servant could be kept, his occupation in the country might be groom or gamekeeper in the morning, and footman and butler in the afternoon. His clothing would be very unconventional. Surtees describes such a man.

> He was attired in a sort of composition dress savouring of the different characters performed. He had on an old white hat, a groom's fustian stable coat cut down into a shooting jacket, red plush smalls [tight breeches] and top boots.
>
> *Jorrocks's Jaunts and Jollities,* 1831–4

A foreigner wrote in 1861, laughing at the way servants in large establishments spent their time:

> . . . the servants in a great house . . . wear white cravats with large faultless bows, scarlet or canary-coloured knee-breeches . . . In the fashionable neighbourhoods, beneath the vestibule, about five o'clock in the evenings the butler seated, newspaper in hand, sips a glass of port; around him, ushers, corded lackeys, footmen with their sticks gaze with an indolent and a lordly air upon the middle-class passers by. The coachmen are prodigiously broad-shouldered and developed . . . These are the favourites of creation, chosen and picked . . . as specimens of the nation's physique.
>
> Taine's *Notes on England*, with an introduction by W. F. Rae, 1872

Charles Bennett in *London People* 1863, also wrote sarcastically about the employment of many servants in wealthy homes:

> I think sometimes that the worst evils in the train of riches are servants. What with the quiet impudence and supercilious civility of *footmen*, the cringing of the ready-willed and as ready-witted *lady's maid*, the hot temper of the *cook*, the dignity of the *butler* and perhaps drunkenness of the *coachman* . . . I really thank Providence sometimes for not having sent me a hundred thousand pounds . . . .

In the end he is sympathetic:

> For how is it possible for any human being habitually to wear a face of impossible vacuity, to assume an air of formal subserviency . . . to bear the gaudy badge of servitude without taking secret revenge upon society which dooms him to such a fate . . . – when the flour and the lard get on to the hair instead of into the piedish – I take it that man is only suited for the place he fills. The plush has subdued his soul to the quality of the Servants' Hall.

CHAPTER TWO

Livery

The Nobles of our Land were much delighted then,
To have at their command a crue of lustie Men:
Which by their Coates were knowne, of Tawnie,
                            Red or Blue,
With Crests on their sleeves showne, when this
                            old Cap was new. (17th century)
        "Times Alteration" *A Century of Ballads*, ed. John Ashton, p. 5

Since livery played such an important part in the costume of all retainers in medieval times and of the lower grade household servants later, a general description will be helpful.

The lower grade liveried servants had their clothes provided. Livery was a style of uniform prescribed for the dress of retainers. In the seventeenth century military and civil uniforms diverged, the latter retaining the name "livery"[1]. Livery was at first worn by all retainers. A duke's son might act as page and many cases are recorded of younger brothers of noblemen serving their elder brothers and wearing their livery. Livery was also worn by common men, who would join as retainers to the nobleman whose livery they wore. So formidable a body did they become that a law was passed permitting the master to give livery only to his own household servants, officers, etc., by licence. Licences and retainers were abolished in Charles II's reign, since when livery has been worn only by the lower ranks of household servants.[2]

Livery garments, in general, were at first more or less in the fashion of their day, but later tended towards an old-fashioned dignity. The materials used for lower ranks were of a heavier and rather coarser make than those for gentlemen servants. There were, however, special features of a livery garment which stamped it as *livery*.

[1] James Laver *Country Life Annual*, 1951.

[2] W. D. F. Vincent *The Cutter's Practical Guide, Part 4, to Livery Garments.*

LIVERY COLOURS

Livery colours, of a noble family, in medieval days, might be worn on occasion by anyone who served the family in any way and this included superior gentlemen servants and even the clergy. The livery colour of Sir John Howard of Stoke by Nayland, was "crimson engrained" (dyed before weaving), bought in bulk. Various qualities were used, according to rank.

> xlj yerdes and iii quarters engreyned, pryse of the yerd, vi s.   1465
>
> *Household Accounts of Sir John Howard* 1463–7
> in *Manners and Household Expenses* . . . Roxburghe Club, 1841

The correct colours were worn in the hat, hood or gown. The main colour and the facings would usually correspond respectively with the two most prominent colours in the family arms.

Crimson livery was also worn by servants and retainers of the Duke of Norfolk in 1465 and even by some of his friends, a custom very much objected to by Henry VII who decreed that livery should be confined to domestic retainers.

In 1455–60 Margaret Paston, in a letter to her husband, was very concerned at not being able to obtain the colours he desired at a reasonable price:

> As touching for your liveries, there can none be gotten here of that colour that ye would have of, neither murrey [purplish red] nor good russet, under 3s. the yard at the lowest price.

In 1522 "tawney orange colour" was chosen for the livery of Sir Thomas Lovell's servants, and scarlet bonnets "Milenfacion at v s the bonnet. Blew clothe bought for my Lorde Earle's servants". (*MSS. of the Duke of Rutland*, Hist. MSS. Commission, 1905.)

Tawney remained also a popular colour for liveries in the sixteenth century.

> 40 yards of tawnie cloth for liveries at viii s the yard and given my retainers.

was ordered in 1577, when Lord North's household was entertaining the Queen. The Lestrange accounts mention white and red for liveries in 1530. Particoloured livery was also sometimes chosen.

The varied colours worn by an Elizabethan page who absconded are listed in an advertisement for his recovery. His doublet was yellow, with peach-coloured buttons and crimson lining. He also had a carnation-coloured cloak and blue stockings. (J. Nichols *Progresses of Queen Elizabeth.*)

Dr. F. G. Emmison tells us in his *Tudor Food and Pastimes* that for the liveried servants at Ingatestone Hall, grey frieze was supplied for winter wear and grey marble for the summer. The grey marble was a particoloured worsted interwoven so as to resemble the veining of marble. But even there, blue was the dominant colour for servants' liveries.

Russet, though mentioned for livery by Margaret Paston, was usually a countryman's colour and a russet coat generally indicated a yokel. From the sixteenth century blue became far the commonest livery colour. Hence, in a satire on the Serving Man's profession written in 1598, we read of an ambitious

> yeoman or husbandman's soune, aspiring from the Plough to the Parlor ... moved him to change his habite and cullour from Jerkin to Coate and from Russett to Blew.
>
> J. M. op cit.

The Duke of Bristol, in 1623, when attending a wedding, had more than thirty "rich liveries made of watchet[1] velvet with silver lace to the very capes of their cloaks". Lace, meaning braid, as a decorative edging to a garment, often of metal thread, was popular from the mid-fifteenth century on.

In Thomas Baker's play *The Fine Lady's Airs*, 1709, the valet remarks to his master:

> You wear lac'd coats. We lac'd Liveries ...
> You pinck Holes with your Swords; we crack sculls
> with our Sticks.

Blue was so widely adopted for livery that a "blue coat" or "blue-aproned man" became the term applied to servants or apprentices (later tradesmen too) from the end of the sixteenth to the eighteenth century. This colour was therefore carefully avoided by gentlemen. Watchet, a coarse blue material, was commonly used for livery coats; but breeches had to be of a different colour. The many references to these blue coats are in a scornful vein. To keep tradesmen in awe,

---

[1]Watchet = blue, or, in some contexts, a kind of blue cloth.

.... if any saucy blue apron dares to affront any venerable person ...
all scholars are immediately forbid to have any dealings with him.

Nicholas Amhurst *Terrae Filius* Essay No. XLIII (1721) Edn. M 26 p. 239

In the seventeenth and eighteenth centuries blue was still the favourite colour for liveries. In Blundell's *Diary and Letter Book* in 1713 he gives an account of a number of livery garments including:

> Blew livery stockings 1–2
> Blew serge for was-cots at 2s 4d per yd.
> Blew serge for facing at 2s per yd.

Even the nineteenth century continued with blue.

> Dark blue livery coat and breeches, striped vest, white stockings and shoes.

These were the instructions for the costume of a servant in Tom Taylor's play *Still Waters Run Deep*, 1855. The nineteenth century also liked yellow. Creevey in 1825 described "six or seven Livery servants in bright yellow dress coats" (*Creevey's Life and Times*, ed. by John Goss), and the instructions for the costume of a servant in George Lovell's play *Look before you leap*, c. 1846, were:

> Drab livery coat trimmed with carpet lace[1]; yellow cloth waistcoat, yellow plush breeches.

Thackeray makes yellow proverbial with his *Yellowflush Papers*, and again:

> Rich liveries – two great footmen with red whiskers and yellow-plush small-clothes.

> *The Great Hoggarty Diamond*, 1849

Since livery colours of old families were fixed by verbal tradition, the *Gentleman's Magazine* in 1784 suggested that "all future editions of the Peerage and Baronetages" should record in print the colours of old families. This was not carried out, but a chart showing the various livery colours of the early nineteenth century can be seen at the Bristol Museum.

Colour schemes were now left to individual choice, but brown must have been uncommon. We are told that in 1821 Lord Petersham, the eccentric dandy, on falling in love with a Mrs. Brown,

> His passion declared itself in the following way. He purchased a brown carriage, brown livery, brown hat, brown spurs – and finally being obliged

[1] Braid.

18

to have an embroidered coat for Court wear he had it in brown, embroidered with dead leaves.

Private Letters of Princess Lieven to Prince Metternich, 1820–1826, ed. P. Quennell [John Murray] 1937

Dickens in *The Pickwick Papers*, 1836–7, gives an account of the startling colours worn by footmen at Bath.

> Powder-headed footman with gorgeous livery.
> In a bright crimson coat with long tails, vividly red breeches and a cocked hat . . . . . .

Another "in a yellow waistcoat . . . ."
Another "in orange-coloured plush . . . ."
Another "in light blue suit with leaden buttons."

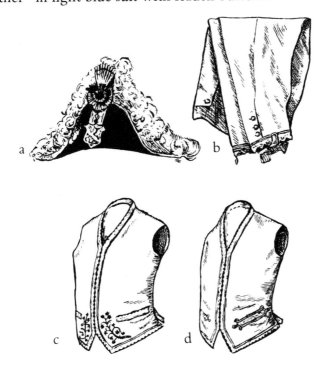

2. Footman's semi-state livery. (a) Cocked hat, full dress, made of silk nap and trimmed with feathers and cockade. (b) Breeches made of yellow plush. (c) Waistcoats, i.e. vests, of dark blue cloth (to match the coat – not shown) the edges trimmed with gold Vandyke lace, one trimmed with a fern-leaf pattern, [1890–5].

Surtees in 1854 has this to say, and is apparently laughing at the livery of a servant dressed in

> a rich blue, green, yellow, red, all the colours of the rainbow reflecting, cut velvet vest [waistcoat] set off with steel buttons; a splendid velvet-collared blue coat and superfine drab trousers with broad brown stripes down the sides.
>
> *Handley Cross*

The free choice proved startling. For example, the ambitious wife of a lawyer, engaging her first footman in 1847, wrote:

> The livery I had made was one of the sweetest things when it was new. Every article of the entire suit was a different colour. I ordered . . . the love of a white coat and a pet of a canary waistcoat, and a perfect duck of a pair of bright crimson plush knee what d'ye callums.
>
> H. & A. Mayhew *The Greatest Plague of Life*

Euphemisms for breeches were numerous from the end of the eighteenth to well into the nineteenth century.

With the introduction of aniline dyes in the 1860's strange results followed, but by the end of the century gaudy colours were not in good taste and the *Tailor and Cutter* of 1897 has a scathing comment on the subject.

> Garments made from every conceivable shade, yellow, green, salmon, blue, plum . . . . . gaudy but ugly, showy but cumbersome, costly and well nigh useless, eccentric if not grotesque. The sooner some of these are presented to family museums the better.

T. H. Holding tells us in 1894:

> The mark of gentility is now to have livery dark in colour, unobtrusive in style, quietly made, without indeed much ornamentation . . . other than that afforded by metal buttons, or a tiny bit of vest that shows above, below, or through the openings of the coat. The drab gaiters of old-fashioned shape and cut have also gone and leather boots with brown tops have taken the place to be worn over white breeches, and the footman wears dark trousers in place of breeches and gaiters.
>
> *Uniforms of British Army, Navy and Court*

In the event of mourning, however, in the nineteenth century, black was correct, but

> if the garments are not made from black, then cloth . . . [black] bands are put on the arm, as well as cuffs and collar . . . These bands are generally put on the left arm just above the elbow, about two inches wide. Some

firms put the band on the right arm for the coachman, and on the left arm for the footman, so that they may look symmetrical when they are seated on the box.

W. D. F. Vincent, *British Livery Garments*, [1890–5]

Livery buttons, too, had to harmonise with the colour of the livery suit, though not necessarily of the same colour. Vincent advised, for example, that if the coachman's coat matched the colour of the body of the carriage, the buttons should be the same colour as the harness fittings.

"Long buttons with silver heads" for blue livery cloaks are listed in 1661 in the Household Books of Sir Miles Stapleton (*The Ancestor*, Vol. 3).

In T. Hughes's *Tom Brown's School Days* (1856) we read of a retired servant "70 years old" living with the Brown family who attended the local fair "resplendent in a long blue coat and brass buttons and a pair of old yellow buckskins and top-boots which he had cleaned for and inherited from Tom's grandfather, a stout thorn stick in his hand and a nosegay of pinks and lavender in his botton-hole".

Crest buttons were used on dress livery breeches only. In the event of mourning the crest buttons would be changed to plain black.

The usual number of buttons required for various garments in the late nineteenth century was as follows:

Overcoat, 18 large
Coachman's frock 12 large, 4 small
Coachman's vest 8 small
Footman's coatee 22 large, 4 small
Footman's vest 4 or 5 small
Groom's frock 10 or 12 large, 4 small
Page's jacket 16 or 18 ball buttons.

W. D. F. Vincent, *op. cit.*

THE LIVERY BADGE

The badge was a mark, token or device worn by servants and retainers as a sign of allegiance. For example, the ragged staff of Beauchamp, Earl of Warwick (Fig. 3), the portcullis of Beaufort or the rising sun of York. Even as early as 1300 a badge of some kind was worn, to show to which household the wearer belonged. In 1240 Henry III ordered

3. (a) Retainer wearing Earl of Warwick's livery badge (ragged staff) on the back of his short jacket, 1485–90. (b) Two of General Monk's watermen wearing their master's badge on their sleeves. 1670.

that livery outdoor garments distributed at Christmas should have "R" worked in red silk on the cloth below the collar.[1]

In medieval times the badge was generally embroidered on the breast, back or sleeve of the servant's outer garment, as shown in Fig. 3(a):

> In 1458 . . . Richard Duke of York lodged here [Baynard Castle] . . . and . . . all his noble partizans had their warlike suite. Let me say, that the King – making earl came attended with six hundred men all in red jackets embroidered with ragged staves before and behind.
>
> Thomas Pennant *Some Account of London*, pp. 368–9 (1790)

From the sixteenth century, the badge might be engraved or embossed on a metal plate affixed to the sleeve. (See Fig. 3(b).)

On Queen Elizabeth I's visit to Lord Ellesmere at Harefield in 1602 expenses included:

[1] Letters of Edward, Prince of Wales (later Ed. II) 1304–5, Hilda Johnstone [Roxburghe Club O.U.P. 1931].

payde to goldsmith for badges xxix li iii s and To Mr. Farrington for liveries cxxiiii li iii d.[1]

When blue became the favourite colour for livery, an employer's family badge could be used to distinguish his livery from others. From *c.* 1560 to 1630's when sham hanging sleeves were fashionable, the badge was blazoned on these. The sham hanging sleeves were pendant streamers attached to the back of the armhole, sometimes on jerkins, but were merely ornamental, being the remains of true hanging sleeves. In *Health to the Gentlemanly Profession of Serving Men*[2] in 1598 we hear of "Tom the Taylor" who went into service and found it

> strange to finde a Blew-coate on his back with *badge* on his sleeve ... But now being kept in his liverie he thinketh himselfe as good a man with the Sheeres at his backe as the Poet Lauret with a penne in his eare.

A badge, representing a *Rose and Crown* was blazoned on the doublets of Queen Elizabeth's attendants, as also on the uniform of the Yeomen of the Guard, instituted by Henry VII

> Crimosyn satten for thembroidering of Roses and crownes ... for the Riche coates of needlecloth for the garde ... crimosyn satten for Roses for iiii s Riding coates for ii yomen of the gard. 1517
> Henry VIII's Wardrobe Book *Archaeologia*, Vol. 9

A Sumptuary Law in 1597 forbade the use of silks to working men, but the following exception was made.

> .... her Ma[ties] servantes and the servantes of noblemen and gentlemen may weare such lyverye coates or clokes as their masters shall give or allowe unto them, with their *badges* and cognizances or other ornamentes of velvet or silke, to be layed or added to [them].
> *The Egerton Papers* ed. J. P. Collier 1840

Fynes Moryson in his Itinerary (1605–17) says:

The servants of gentlemen were wont to weare blew coates with their Masters *badge* of silver on the left sleeve, but now they most commonly weare clokes garded [trimmed, edged] with lace, all the servants of one family wearing the same liverie for colour and ornament ....

1611–12

---

[1] *The Egerton Papers* from the original mss, the property of the Rt. Hon. Lord Francis Egerton, M.P., ed. J. P. Collier (Camden Soc., 1840).
[2] Shakespeare Assoc. 1931.

4. Two grooms who stand at head and rear of the horse have the livery badge of rose and crown blazoned on the front of their doublets. They wear fashionable trunk hose like the chief huntsman kneeling before Queen Elizabeth and demonstrating "the goodnesse of the [deer's] flesh", 1575.

In the Household Accounts of the Earl of Rutland, 1611–12, we find peacocks used as badges.

> Blew coates and cocks . . . Peacockes imbrodered for liverys, the grounds Velvett for gentlemen costs vis the peece, and the groundes sattin for yeomen costs vs the peece.
>
> *MSS. of the Duke of Rutland*, IV, p. 486

Badges were also worn by gentlemen retainers in ceremonial livery – that is before Charles II's reign, when, as already stated, livery became the rule for lower grade servants only. Many liveried gentlemen are mentioned in *The Diary of Henry Machyn, 1550–60* (ed. by John G. Nichols, Camden Soc.):

> The XVII day of Feybruary th'erle of Pembroke cam rydyng in to London with iiic horse, and after hym a C gentyllmen with chanes of gold, all in blew cloth plane with a badge on ther sleeve, a dragon and so to Bernard Castle, and ther he leyff [lives].

Vincent tells us that

> The badge was probably peculiar to England, as it appears to have excited the curiosity of foreigners in the time of Queen Elizabeth.
>
> *Op. cit.* [1890–5]

Although servants' livery badges were widely in evidence up to and during the sixteenth century, they gradually ceased to be used except in special cases, for example, on the tabards of heralds, and by the Lord Mayor's servants.

Another kind of badge was adopted in the eighteenth century and this was known as the *Shoulder Knot*. It consisted of a bunch of ribbon, cord or braid loops, sometimes bejewelled, sometimes finished with decorative metal tags called aiglets, and from 1660 to 1700 was worn by gentlemen as an ornament dangling from the right shoulder. But after that date it became part of livery and "a Knight of the Shoulder Knot" meant a footman. A curious attempt was once made thus to hall-mark women servants, as it was not always evident from the costume which was mistress and which was maid.

> If the mistress be not known, it is no easy matter to distinguish her from her maid.   1772
>
> Pierre Jean Grosley, *A Tour to London or New Observations on England and its Inhabitants* (2 Vols)

5. Livery collar. The SS collar of the Lancastrians.

Much to their dismay, women servants in 1729 heard a rumour that "the Queen intends to cause a Bill to be brought in" not only to limit their wages, but "that women servants shall wear a sort of shoulder knot of the colour of the footman's liveries belonging to such a family . . ." (*Viscount Percival's Diary* for 1729). Needless to say, the bill did not become law.

LIVERY COLLARS

The livery collar, at first a badge of service, became the collar of an order of honorary distinction such as the collar of Esses or SS collar which was the livery collar of the House of Lancaster installed by John of Gaunt, *c.* 1360. An Ordinance of 1478 stated:

> Item, that every lord and knight within the household weare a collar of the kinges livery about his necke as to him apperteyneth, and that every squire, as well squires for the bodie as other of the household, likewise weare collers of the kinges liverie daylie about their neckes as to them apperteyneth, and that none of the said squires faile, upon paine of loosing a monethes wages. (1)
> Household of Edward IV, *The Black Book and Ordinance of 1478*, ed. A. R. Myers, Manchester University Press 1958, p. 205

The collars of the Orders of Knighthood symbolize allegiance in a similar way, but allegiance to a group, an ideal, instead of to a master.

---

[1] Quoted by W. O. Hassall in *How They Lived, 55 B.C. – 1485*.

LIVERY HEAD WEAR

From the Middle Ages up to the seventeenth century when it was customary for some kind of head gear to be worn indoors as well as out, it was laid down that not even a high ranking servant might have his head covered when in attendance on his master, though very occasionally a coif was allowed. Out of doors, hats worn with livery were often plumed. (See Fig. 3(a), 1485.)

Striking hats and caps were very fashionable in Tudor times and "every servyng man . . . even all indifferently dooe weare of these hattes". (P. Stubbes, *Anatomie of Abuses*, 1585.)

The flat cap, which had a flat crown, spreading over a flat narrow brim and made of wool, was introduced by Henry VIII. By 1570 it was by order being worn by citizens and apprentices and discarded by the gentry. It became known as the City flat cap, but by mid-seventeenth century was only seen as a livery head dress (see Fig. 6). Strange to say, in the early seventeenth century some of the aristocracy insisted that, as a mark of respect, the coachman should drive them without his hat on. It is recorded that at his fall Lord Bacon was censured for this practice.

Livery hats, in the eighteenth century especially, were generally expensive and very grand, being also selected for display. They were of the "tricorne" shape, but the material and decorations were carefully chosen. In 1742 Elizabeth Purefoy wrote to Charles Meredith, a London hatter:

> I desire you will send me two Caroline Hats of a fashionable size for the servants. Let them be so good as to be serviceable . . . let each of them be laced with a gold lace . . . and to have gold loops and gold Buttons. It must be gold of both sides and not a gaws lace.[1]

All this "for ye Livery hats".

A Caroline hat was made of beaver fur, imported from Carolina and inferior to the Canadian fur known as "French Beaver". Caroline hats therefore were cheaper and generally worn by servants. These hats were usually black.

The Journal of Timothy Burrell, Esq., has the following entry for June, 1711:

> My two servants' liveries cost £6.6s. their lace hats £1.1.6d
> > *Sussex Archaeological Collections* III

[1] Gauze lace, i.e. braid which had a ground of plain net.

In Blundell's Diary, a price list of what was spent on livery is given, and this includes:

Two hats for my livery servants 5 – 0.

Silver lace for my livery hats 15 – 0. 1713

By the end of the century the "tricorne" cocked hat was going out of fashion, being replaced by what was called the "round hat". This had a tall crown and varying-sized brim which became increasingly narrower, forecasting the top hat of the nineteenth century.

In a play, *The Way to get Married* by Thomas Morton, 1796, the costume instructions for a servant were:

old fashioned livery, and large cocked hat.

Cockades were first worn in England in the first quarter of the eighteenth century.

The black cockade . . . was the Hanoverian badge, and was adopted in contradistinction to the white cockade of the House of Stuart by all officers of the Army and Navy in direct service of the Crown; their servants wore them also, to show that though not in uniform, they were soldiers and sailors, and as time went on, the private servants of officers in the two services adopted them . . . .

Cockades are of three sorts:

1. *The Royal Cockade* which is quite round and made of flexible leather . . . .
2. *The Military Cockade* – This is oval, made of stiff leather, and ornamented with a fan or comb. Worn by servants of officers of the army or navy . . . .
3. *The Naval or Civil Cockade* – The same as the last, but without the fan. Worn by servants of naval officers or the Diplomatic Corps etc. . . . .

W. D. F. Vincent, *op. cit.*

Vincent also describes how the cockade should be attached to the hat.

The cockade is put on by the aid of a hairpin and a cork. First find the position desired (always on the left side) (the fan part of the cockade should come above the crown); then two holes are made in the side of the hat, and the hairpin put through cockade and hat, and fastened over a cork on the inside. Livery silk hats are heavier than the ordinary style and are made more with the view of exposure to bad weather than the ordinary kind . . . Hats sometimes have silver lace binding and band, in which case the bow of the band comes in the front.

From the mid-nineteenth century top hats were correct, worn with their evening dress-like uniform by butlers and by any male servant in livery. (Pl. 1(a).)

Livery

The cost of supplying handsome livery for gentlemanly serving men was often very, very great. An entertaining account of a nobleman's difficulty on this score, when he had to present himself at Court before the King, has come down to us in the writing of a gentlemanly serving man, recollecting his past experience in the reign of Henry VIII. He stated that the price of everything had gone up three times since his youth, and this amounted to a very large sum when it was thought necessary to have this "costly apparell" such as "cloth of Gold, of Silver, Velvet, Sattin, Taffata, or such like ware . . . amounting in one yeere to more than the revenues of his lands". Then he goes on to say:

> Concerning this costly and fashionate apparel, I remember a notable example of a King of England . . . that calling upon occasion certain of his Noblemen and Peeres of his Realme to the Court, whyther when they came, one amongst them came very homely appareled, in a jerkin of frieze and a payre of breeches of countreys Russet and attendantes were a hundred or five score proper and personable men, all well horsed and gallantly furnished at all poyntes.

Whereupon the King praised the troupe of attendants, but rebuked the nobleman for being himself

> apparelled in so base and unseemly a suit saying I cannot but highly discommend, for that it befitteth not a man of your estate . . . but always to be apparelled in costly, comely, decent and handsome habit.

The nobleman then retired and told his man to go and buy him

> a rich gown of blacke velvet, the sleeves thereof all beset with Aglets of Gold, a Velvet Cappe, with a fether and a golde Bande, very richly bordered about with Pearles and precious stones of great value, a suite of cloth of golde of the newest and richest fashion.

Thus richly furnished, attended with only one Man and a Page, he presented himself before the King the next morning.

> You are now like yourself said the King, and as you should be, but where is your goodly trayne of Men and horse wherewith you were yesterday so gallantly garded.

The nobleman replied by throwing off his cap and his

> sumptuous rayment saying that all his Men and Horses were turned into gorgeous garments.

He could not afford both for himself and his troupe, which would the King prefer – obviously a modestly clothed nobleman with a

troupe of Horse and Men, to do your master's service at home or abroad against your Grace's foreign foes.

"I.M." *A Health to the Gentlemanly Profession of Serving Men* 1598

From the mid-nineteenth century, there was a general decline in the wearing of livery. The reason is explained by Mayhew in his *London Characters*, 1874.

The 19th century considers livery a badge of servitude . . . certain it is a man for livery [i.e. a servant in the lower ranks] is scarcer than he was . . . In what one called single-handed places, it is even more difficult to get a man to wear livery . . . He likes . . . to consider himself on the level of a butler.

By the end of the century the day of the picturesque servant was coming to an end and household servants had to conform to hygiene, convenience and democracy.

Since the Yeomen of the Guard eventually became household retainers of the reigning sovereign they may be added to our list of servants in livery.

The Yeomen of the Guard was at first a military corps in attendance on the sovereign, and created by Henry VII in 1485. However, from the reign of Queen Elizabeth I they ceased to be a fighting force, and became personal body guards in the household of the reigning sovereign. Their original duties were most comprehensive and in Tudor times included the making of the King's bed. Each portion was separately examined. Another of their later duties was the searching of the vaults of the Houses of Parliament, dating from the "Gunpowder Plot" in 1605.

The uniform or livery in Tudor times was a red tunic with purple facings and stripes and gold lace ornaments, red-knee-breeches, red stockings (white in Georgian period) a flat black hat with a red, white and blue band, and black shoes with red, white and blue rosettes. The Stuarts replaced the ruff and round hats with lace and plumed hats. Queen Anne discarded both ruff and lace, but retained the flat hats. The ruff was re-introduced by the Georges and has remained as part of the permanent dress of the Yeomen's. Gold embroidered emblems on the back and front of the coats were added. From 1485 till 1603 these were the Tudor crown with the Lancastrian rose and the initials of the reigning sovereign. The Stuarts substituted the St. Edward's crown for the Tudor, and added under it "Dieu et mon Droit". Queen Anne restored the Tudor crown and added the thistle to the rose on the

6. Yeomen of the Guard wearing flat caps, stand on either side of King William and Queen Mary. They have livery badges W.R. (Wm. Rex) on the front of their "vests" (the rose and crown was omitted here). This vest had a collarless bodice, comfortably fitting to the waist with a skirt flowing loosely to the knees. It was a short-lived fashion, coming in soon after 1665, but something similar persists with the Yeomen to the present day. Halberds carried. 1689.

official union with Scotland in 1709. The Georges reverted to the St. Edward's crown and in 1801, on the union with Ireland, added the shamrock to the thistle and rose. Edward VII again changed the St. Edward's crown for the Tudor.

The early military service pikes were carried, and later other weapons of war, but when the Yeomen became the sovereign's household guard they each carried a steel gilt halberd with a tassel of red and gold. (See Fig. 6, 1689.)

It should be noted that the Tower Warders, an offshoot of the Yeomen of the Guard, ceased to be household retainers when the Tower was given up as a royal residence in Henry VIII's reign.

7. Parlour maid, plain gown with short sleeves, chemise sleeves emerging, but no ruffles (frills) as worn by the lady. A mob cap tied under the chin with "kissing strings". Long apron. Black page wearing the usual turban and silver collar probably enbraved with his master's name and address, 1743.

8. Black slave's child. "On one occasion Miss Ophelia found Topsy with her very best scarlet Indian Coniton crepe shawl wound round her head for a turban", 1852.

A Negro Maid, aged about 16 years, much pitted with Small Pox, speaks English well, having a piece of her left Ear bit off by a Dog and she hath on a strip'd Stuff Wastcoat and Petticoat.
Quoted by John Ashton, *Social Life in the Reign of Queen Anne* Vol I, p. 81

9. Black footman in tail coat with shoulder knot, dark breeches and white stockings. The small chimney sweep remarks: "Bob aint you glad you aint a Black-amoor", 1834–6.

As already stated, this unhappy state of affairs came to an end in the mid-nineteenth century.

CHAPTER THREE

Dress in general

ACQUISITION OF CLOTHING

Some servants had certain garments in annual contract and some were wholly provided for, but gifts of clothes to supplement wages are mentioned from the Middle Ages on, and this continued into the nineteenth century, whether ordinary garments or livery.

In the Howard Household Account Books,[1] 1463–67, one Thomas Thorpe was given in 1465 "a payre hosene . . . j peyre of botuys [boots] and a payre pynsons [slippers]," and the kitchen maid was given some shoes: "Maude of the Kechen Schone viii d" and for an outside servant, such as a carpenter it is stated that "he schal have fore the yere for wages iiij marc. and a gowne" while the "sawere . . . that schal be wyth my mastyr a yere . . . schal have for wages XLVJ s viij d, and a gowne and his beddynge". 1467

The Howards' Noblemen retainers were supplied with crimson gowns, the quality depending on the rank of the recipient. John Dee's Diary in 1594 states:

> I did pay Lettice her full year's wages . . . being four nobles, an apron and a pair of hose and shoes.
> *English Diaries XVI, XVII, XVIII centuries*, ed. by J. Aitken 1941

The Willoughby Accounts give us more examples. In 1527

> Item a payre of Schowne for Lytyll John of the kechyn vi d.
> Item for a pere of hosen for hym vi d . . . a cape . : . x d.

In 1573 the "kitchen boy" was supplied with jerkin, doublet and breeches which were made to measure. "Fryce" [a napped woollen cloth] was ordered for another servant for his winter livery.

Certainly the cost of clothes, especially when supplied for important

---

[1] In Roxburghe Club publication, 1841.

occasions, could be very great for the noble lord. At the marriage of James I's daughter, later Queen of Bohemia, in 1613 we read:

> Your Honour made 81 clokes for your seruants and those of the kitchen had five yards a peece allowed them. Theis clothes came to £263 od monie [about].
>
> F. Grose *Antiquarian Repertory* Vol. I

In the Earl of Bedford's steward's accounts, in 1670–81, a number of articles of clothing are recorded, such as stockings, hats, cuff buttons, shoe buckles and also for the little page:

> For two shirts for the little page 7s. 6d.
> For two periwigs for my lady's page £2.0.0.

However, part of the cost of his clothing had to be paid for by the servant himself.

The cost of supplying garments was also sometimes rather troublesome. In October, 1666, Pepys wrote of a new waiting maid they were engaging.

> She is wretched poor, and but ordinary favoured; and we fain to lay out seven or eight pounds worth of clothes upon her back, which, methinks, do go against my heart.

So by now apparently it was not always obligatory to provide clothing for all servants.

Some farm servants, in the seventeenth century, expected to be supplied with clothes on being engaged for service.

> Some . . . condition to have an olde suite, a payre of breeches, an olde hatte and a payre of shoes; and mayde servants to have an apron, smocke or both.
>
> *Rural Economy in Yorkshire in 1641*, ed. C. B. Robinson, 1857

Such was the second-hand clothing demanded by Yorkshire farm employees.

Parson Woodforde in 1781 tells us that he

> before breakfast walked to Lewis's shop and there bought 6 yds. of printed linen for my under Maid at 2/2 per yard

and in 1785 he agreed to take on a farmer's son aged about 13, as a new servant, being well recommended. Then he says:

> I gave the Boy by way of earnest Money 0.1.0. I am to give him per annum for Wages 1.1.0. a Coat and Waistcoat and Hat when wanted, to allow him

something for being washed out and mended – and his friends to find him in Stockings and Shoes . . . .

One hopes that he had plenty of friends!

In 1785 the parson paid £1. 1. 0. to his taylor for

making two suits of Frocks[1] and waistcoats for my new Man and new Boy, Buttons, Pockets, Thread etc. included.

In 1789 he gave his "two Maids a Cotton Gown apiece, that I bought for them in London cost me 1. 8. 0." and in 1791 he wrote:

Betty went to Norwich to buy my two old Washerwomen . . . a new gown apiece which I intend giving to them.

The Diary of a Country Parson. The Rev. James Woodforde, 1758–1802, Vol. III

Servants who had to wear livery were generally supplied with new clothes when taking service. This was the custom from medieval days on. It did not, however, mean that the garments belonged to these servants. In a sense they were only lent to them, as shown by Parson Woodforde's statement in 1785:

My Man Briton had a new suit of Livery brought home this Evening from Norwich with very good new great Coat of Brown Cloth and red Cape to it. I told Briton that I gave neither to him, but only to wear them during his service with me.

Ibid. Vol. II, p. 212

Livery, of course, had to be renewed from time to time, and the cost of new clothes was beyond the purse of the ordinary servant. The following rather pathetic letter was written to Lady Stafford in 1740 by her gamekeeper.

I humbly beg your ladyship will be pleased to consider my clothing, for walking about the park and woods I am got as ragged as a sheep; its upwards of two years since I had any, and my lord was pleased to be so good as tell me I should have a frock every year and a plush coat every tow [two] years, and a laced hatt as other noblemen's keepers had.

Joseph Wilkinson, *Worthies, Families and Celebrities of Barnsley and the District* 1883

For servants working in a household where death had occurred, mourning garments were provided (pl. 30). In 1585 John Lennard spent a considerable sum on mourning at the death of his wife.

---

[1] An eighteenth-century frock was an "undress" coat with a turn-down collar.

Clothes for relations and servants £76.18.8.
Men servants cloaks 4 yds at 16/– a yd.
Women's gowns 3 yards at 13/4 a yd.

Then again in 1694, provided for mourning was

> A black coat lin'd with crape and black waistcoate of crape, also to make his man a coat of ordinary black cloath and line it with Shaloon[1] – a pair of black worsted stockins and a fashionable mourning hat band; cloth crape 2/5 a yard. Black cloth 12/– a yd.
>
> *Accounts of the Families of Lennard and Barrett, (1585–1694)*
> Holly Trees Museum, Colchester. (privately printed) 1908.

Samuel Pepys in 1667 on the death of his mother wrote:

> and my two under-mayds . . . give them hoods and scarfs and gloves.

which were the conventional garments worn at a funeral. Again, the personal account book of Lady Arabella Furnese [North MSS., U471 – A50] which is preserved among North MSS., Kent County Archives, Maidstone, states:

> For black gloves, fans and girdles for all the women servants.   1721

Similar mourning attire is described by the Parson Woodforde at a funeral in 1780:

> Attended by two servant maids in very deep mourning and long black hoods . . . .
> The Drivers and other Servants had hat bands tied with white Love-Ribband[2] and a pair of white Gloves.
>
> *The Diary of a Country Parson*, Vol. I

An interesting order for mourning is given by an economical lady (of fiction) in 1820:

> I beg you will go to Baillie Delap's shop and get swatches[3] of his best black bombaseen and crape and muslin and bring them over to the manse . . .
> I requeesht that on this okasion ye'll get the very best the Baillie has . . .
> You will get likewise swatches of mourning print, with the lowest prices.

---

[1] A slight woollen stuff, much used for linings of men's coats.
[2] Love was a thin silk, and the love-ribbon was a decoration worn as a symbol of loyalty.
[3] Samples, patterns.

I'll be no particular about them as they are for the servant lasses, and there's no need for all the greatness of God's gifts that we should be wasteful.

John Galt, *The Ayrshire Legatees* or *The Pringle Family* Letter VI, Mrs. Pringle to Molly Glencairn.

Sylvia's Home Journal in 1879 has this to say:

All servants should have black dresses, black shawls, and black bonnets. It is customary to give servants mourning when an important member of the family dies.

BEQUESTS

Other sources of supply of clothes were those bequeathed in wills. These garments would always be meant for the higher ranking personal domestics.

An early example in the first quarter of the thirteenth century is the will of Agnes de Clifford who bequeathed to her servant Matild: "A scarlet robe, an embroidered collar and a bedspread" as well as ten marks.

A surgeon's will in 1591 left to his trusted servant (the category is not stated) the following:

To John Dighton my servaunte my black cloth cloake layed with lace and faced valvet, my blacke satten Doublet and my rounde hose.[1]
Quoted by Sidney Young in *Annals of the Barber-Surgeon* (1890)

We are told that the poet Gray left all his "wearing apparel and linen" by will to his servant.

Upper servants also would sometimes bequeath garments to servants who had worked under them. This is the will of a Steward in 1582:

To Thomas Peereson an apprentice . . . two or three pairs of old and new shoes, my old nether stockings . . . .
To my servant if he be with me at the time of my decease, one of my best tawney livery coats, a good felt hat, handruffs and my rapier.
To John Kemp, the boy of my Master's kitchen an old hat, a black cap, two pairs of handruffs.
Will of William Markaunt of St. Giles, Colchester

Women too were frequently remembered. Margaret Paston in her will dated February 4th, 1482, left

[1] Trunk hose, the usual leg wear of that date.

to Agnes Swan, my servant, my musteredevelys[1] gown, furred with blak, and a girdell of blak harneised with silver gilt and enamelled, and xx s in money.

And Sarah, Duchess of Marlborough, directed in her will that her wardrobe was to be distributed to her lady's maid and two other maid servants. (Colville, *Duchess Sarah*, p. 373.)

CAST-OFFS

As with garments left in wills, so those given as cast-offs were supplied to top ranking servants, hence the elegance of valets and ladies' maids. Lady Newton, in her epilogue to the *Lyme Letters 1660–1760* tells us that a butler, applying for a situation at Lyme, which he is anxious to obtain, accepts the post, in spite of low wages as he is glad to hear that he is to have Mr. Legh's old clothes. Again, in *Memoirs of an Eighteenth Century Footman*, his master tells him:

"I shall give you my old clothes if you please me". The same applied to the women. Lord Bristol commended his son for having turned out Lady Bristol's personal effects for her maid, "Williams":

> I am glad to find you have delivered to Williams all the things which were your poor mother's and which by a customary sort of right are now become due to every common servant in her place.
> *Letter Books of John Hervey* Vol. III 1726–50

The wages of a wet nurse were also supplemented by second-hand garments, somewhat refurbished in order to please her. We read:

> Mrs Kennet the nurse will soon be restored to her husband. We are to make up her salary to £50. I have given her a good deal of clothes too, the brown silk night gown, [in fact it was an 'undress' day gown] a brown camblet[2], two short cotton gowns, and I have dyed my purple Tabby blue, and added two yards of new to it which will make her fine. 1744
> *Elizabeth Montagu – The Queen of the Blue Stockings* Vol. I, ed. E. J. Clemenson 1900

In 1790 Parson Woodforde records passing on a number of garments:

> Gave my Clark James Smith, a good black striped Coat and Waistcoat, a pair of old Velveret Breeches and a powdered Wig . . . .

[1] A woollen cloth woven in Montivilliers in Normandy.
[2] Material of wool or silk or hair, mixed.

The parson was evidently very pleased with the result as later he writes:

James looked very well at Church with the Coat and Waistcoat etc. I gave him Friday.

> *The Diary of a Country Parson, The Rev. James Woodforde* (Vol. III 1788–1792)

Again:

How gentell he a valet looks in his master's old clothes.   1780
> *Tony Lumpkin* (a Play) by J. O'Keeffe

THEFT

Theft of clothes was another way for a servant to better himself. In Timothy Burrell's *Journal and Account Book* the following statement occurs in 1698:

26 April. Thomas Goldsmith came as footman at 30s per an. wages, and a livery coat and waistcoat once in two years, when he was to have a new one; but being detected in theft, I turned him away.

Thomas came back in 1703, starving, and his master was sorry for him so he

paid sharp for his shoos 4s, for making a waistcoat 2s, stockings 1s 6d. breeches 3s. 6d. hat 4s.

An extensive theft of clothes and other articles was announced in May, 1658, in *Mercurius Politicus*. The garments were stolen by a lady's maid who did

steal away from her ladies house . . . .
taking a mingle-coloured wrought Tabby gown of Deer colour and white, a black striped sattin Gown with four broad bone-black silk Laces and a plain black watered [shot] French Tabby Gown; also one Scarlet-coloured and one other Pink-coloured Sarcenet Petticoat skirt died, a white watered Tabby Waistcoat[1], plain; several Sarcenet, . . . thin black Hoods and Scarfs, several fine Holland shirts, a laced pair of Cuffs . . . one pair of Pink-coloured worsted stockings . . . She went away in a greyish Cloth Waist-coat, turned, and a pink-coloured Paragon[2] upper Peticoat with a Green Tammy under one.

[1] A woman's waistcoat at this date was the bodice worn with the petticoat, meaning skirt.
[2] A double camlet which was, at this date "half silk, half hair".

43

This girl also stole a leather bag, presumably to carry away some of her large hoard. As usual a reward was offered for her capture.

The employer's clothes were usually stolen, not to wear, but to sell, and thereby to add to wages.

A servant in 1759 makes this statement:

I have been disposing of some of his Honour's Shirts and other Linnen, which it is a shame his Honour should wear any longer

and another adds:

I shall dispose of my Wardrobe tomorrow.

> From *High Life Below Stairs, a Farce in Two Acts* by the Rev. James Townley

If a servant ran away, since his livery and his clothes, or at least some of them, were the property of his master, this would be considered as an act of theft, as already mentioned in the section about black servants. Therefore advertisements for the recovery of these fugitives were fairly frequent. The *Ipswich Journal* of 1765 had this advertisement:

Servant absconded [wearing] his own brown short hair; buckskin breeches, white swanskin lapelled waistcoat light-coloured cloth cape-coat.

Swanskin was a thick twilled flannel used by working men. The cape coat was an overcoat with a cape collar. Perhaps this man was more wanted for himself than for the clothes he wore. Another advertisement in the same paper was for a

Servant Run away in a brown clipt wig a duffel [coarse woollen] coat, a drill Frock.

The wig may have had some value. It should be noted that even when wigs were *de rigueur* for almost everyone, older men servants in modest households might wear natural hair. See Hogarth's portrait of his servants.

(Pl. 5, also Pl. 13d). For further remarks on the wearing of wigs see p. 89.

BRIBERY

Bribery was again another method of securing clothes. Women responded readily to bribery if the bribe consisted of elegant clothes far superior to what a servant usually wore. A young mistress in 1600, being anxious to have news of her lover, ordered her maid to go to

London to find out about him. Lest the maid should hesitate she offers her clothes:

> Do this and I will give thee for thy pains
> My cambric apron and my Romish gloves,
> My purple stockings and a stomacher.
> Say wilt thou do this Sybil for my sake?

The maid answers enthusiastically:

> Will I quot 'a . . . By my troth yes, I'll go –
> A cambric apron, gloves, a pair of purple stockings and a stomacher! I'll sweat in purple, mistress for you . . .
>> Thomas Dekker, *The Shoemaker's Holiday* II, iii (1600)

The maid's own apron would have been made of worsted or cotton which at this date was a woollen cloth of which the nap had been "cottoned" or raised. In this century cambric was a very fine quality linen.

Another example of a bribe or tip given to a servant maid is shown in G. Farquhar's *The Recruiting Officer*, 1706.

> Lucy [the maid] says:
> Indeed, Madam, the last bribe I had was from the Captain and that was only a small piece of Flanders [lace] edging for pinners.

The pinner was a flat circular indoor cap with a frill. Some had streamers known as lappets.

Was the following a form of bribery on the part of servants who expected money in exchange for a gift?

> My Lorde usith . . . to gyfe . . . to his iii Hanshmen [Henchmen] uppon New-Years-Day when they doo gyfe his Lordschip Glovis to his New-Yers-gyft and in rewarde . . . VIs viii to every of them.
>> Earl of Northumberland's Household Book 1512–1525
>> F. Grose ed. *Antiquarian Repertory* Vol. 4

CLEANLINESS AND DEPORTMENT

Throughout these centuries servants were ordered or advised as to how to keep clean. In some types of work, in some periods, it must have been difficult. As has been seen, the cost of washing his clothes was sometimes part of the servant's wages.

In *c.* 1465 a waiter is given this advice, not only regarding cleanliness, but also about deportment.

> 57   For the Wayting Servant
> Apparell thee after thy degree
>   Youth should be *cleane* by kynde:
> Pryde and disdayne goes before,
>   And shame fastnes behynde.
>
> Beholde not thy selfe in thy Apparell,
>   In church ne in streete;
> To gase on thy selfe, men will thinke
>   it is a thing vnmeete.
>
> *Babees Book:* Book of Nurture of Hugh Rhodes and John Russell

Again :—

> Looke, suche clothyng as thou shall weere
> Keepe hem as clenly as thou can;
> And all the Remenant of thy geere,
> For clothyng ofte maketh man.
>
> *Book of Precedence* (E.E.T.S. Extra ser.) 1–10

10. Anglo-Saxons at dinner being served by "gentilmen yomen", kneeling and wearing short, elegant tunics embroidered round the skirt and wrist. Neat, clean shaven and short hair, bare-headed. Eleventh century.

11. A humble family, a forester with wife and daughter at table. A server approaches, wearing a countryman's "jump" drawn in with a belt but has the typical waiter's napkin over his shoulder, and is bare-headed, 1665.

Sir John Harrington, one time tutor to James I's daughter, Elizabeth, suggested some rules for the good management of servants, such as a fine of 6d. for a dirty shirt worn on Sunday (!) or a missing button.

In 1450–60, Bishop Grosseteste's Household Statues give a list of commandments to servants, starting with the command that all servants should serve truly God and their master. The seventh commandment orders the "gentilmen yomen and others" to wear their robes in their master's presence and when serving at table and they must not wear old robes or dirty old shoes. *Babees Book* etc., p. 328–9.

In Shakespeare's *Taming of the Shrew* orders were given by the head man in preparation for the return of their master with his bride.

> Let their blue coats [be] brushed and their garters indifferently [plainly] knit
> and let them wear their new fustian and their white stockings. 1596–7

Here is an account of an effort, in 1605, to smarten up "Pipkin", a general manservant. Mrs. Arthur, his mistress, expecting guests to dinner, addresses her maid:

> Where's that knave Pipkin? . . . .
> Bid the fellow . . .
> Make himself handsome, get him a clean band [collar]. . . .
> Meid:
> Indeed forsooth, mistress, he is such a sloven
> That nothing will be handsome about him!
> He had a pound of soap to scour his face,
> And yet his brow looks like the chimney-stock.

A little later Mrs. Arthur addresses Pipkin:

> Get a napkin and a trencher and wait today.

and tells him to give a napkin and a trencher to Hugh, the manservant of one of the guests, adding

> Hugh, . . .
> Wait at your master's elbow.
> *How a Man may Choose a good Wife from a bad*, Act III sc. iii
> by J. Cooke? in *Dodsley's Old Plays*, ed. W. C. Hazlitt Vol. 9

In December 1681 the Earl of Bedford's Steward makes this entry in his Account Book:

> To the page, for scouring his clothes 1s, od.

In the 18th century scents were lavishly used, often to counteract disagreeable smells. Presumably to sit in the coach behind a perspiring driver and postillion was unpleasant and could be overcome thus:

> Have you pulvilled the coachman and postilion that they may not stink?
> W. Congreve *The Way of the World*

Pulvil was a perfumed powder, hence "pulvilled".

Daniel Defoe, in 1725, with the pen-name of Footman, wrote a poem called *Servitude* with a Postscript giving this advice and headed:

Neatness

> But hithertoo, we've only had Respect
> To what concerns the Mind or Intellect:
> 'Tis true internal Qualities conduce
> To greater Ends, and are of greater Use,
> Than those which only serve for outward Show,
> As powder'd Wiggs, clean Shirts and such like do:
> Yet these are necessary, and 'tis fit,

That those whom Time and Business will permit
Appear before their Masters always clean and neat,
But dont ye run into affected Ways
And apish Gestures practis'd now-a-days.

Alas, the man servant here described did not follow the above advice.

He has the assurance to appear at the sideboard, in a pair of filthy *nankeen breeches* made to fit so extremely tight that a less curious observer might have mistaken them for no breeches at all.

Edward Moore, *The World*, 1755

An interesting description in 1784 of a Frenchman's impression of the duties of English servants regarding cleanliness is worth quoting in full:

In general, the English have many more servants than we have, but more than half of them are never seen – kitchen-maids, stable-men, maidservants in large numbers – all of them being required in view of the high standard of cleanliness. Every Saturday, for instance, it is customary to wash the whole house from attic to basement, outside and in. These servants constitute the main part of the employers' expenses: they are boarded according to general custom and the food required is immense – they never leave the table and there is a supply of cold meat, tea and punch from morning till night . . . .
A Frenchman in England, being the Mélanges sur l'Angleterre of François de la Rochefoucauld 1784, Ed. by Jean Marchand, translated by S. C. Roberts

Contrasting with the Frenchman's impression of England we have a very different account of Scottish servants, as given by Jonathan Gray when he visited Scotland in 1810.

My dear Mary,
With respect to the Scotch, I am more than ever struck with their general dirtiness. The women servants (even at Dr. Buchanan's and other respectable families) go without stockings and many women without shoes. We often see on the road men and women barefoot carrying their shoes in their hands to save the leather. The women are remarkably attentive to their heads, their caps are beautifully clean even when the rest of their dress is filthy: and the younger women who wear no caps have their hair carefully plaited and fastened with a comb.

We saw at Edinburgh the interesting sight of the women treading upon clothes in a bucket to wash them, naked to the middle of the thigh.
The Papers and Diaries of a York Family 1764–1839 ed. Mrs Edwin Gray

12. Washerwoman. Her apron is worn under the typical working woman's jacket bodice which is pink, the skirt green. Mob cap with blue ribbon. She wears pattens to keep her feet off the wet floor, 1816.

Servants working with bare feet, a fact which astonished Jonathan Gray in 1810, seems to have been usual in Scotland at this time. A Mrs. Pringle, a Scottish lady, in a letter written in 1820, has this to say about English servants.

> The servant lasses I cannot abide: they dress better at their work than ever I did . . . and this very morning I saw madam the kitchen lass, mounted on a pair of pattens washing the plain stenes before the door; na, for that matter, a bare foot is not to be seen within the four walls of London, at the least I have na seen no such thing.
> *The Ayrshire Legatees* by John Galt, Letter VI

The pattens referred to were overshoes consisting of wooden soles secured by leather straps and commonly worn by domestics and country folk, though not often without shoes or boots, to raise the wearer out of the dirt. According to Betsy Sheridan, Sheridan's sister, pattens were essentially a low-class footwear in her day. When staying at Bath in 1789 she wrote:

> Our weather is damp and dirty but does not confine us, as you know, we Ladies here trot about in Pattens, a privilage granted nowhere else to genteel women.
> *Betsy Sheridan's Journal* Letters 1784–1786 Ed. by Wm. Lefanu

In the 19th century stress was laid on the wearing of clean aprons after dirty work was completed. A housemaid was told, in 1825, that she must change her dirty apron, after cleaning the fireplace, for a clean one to make the beds in. (S. & S. Adams *The Complete Servant*.)

SLAVES OF FASHION

Fashion, though Folly's child, and guide of fools
Rules e'en the wisest, and in learning rules.
George Crabbe *The Library* (1781), l. 167

In spite of sumptuary laws against extravagance, domestic servants, all through these centuries liked to dress in the fashion and avoid clothes suggestive of "low class". Masters too, in the days of liveried servants, liked to display their wealth and status on the backs of their retainers.

Taking men servants first, we find, as early as the fifteenth century, a song that expresses this point of view.

Of servynge men I wyll begyne
For they goo mynyon trym
Off mete and drynk, and feyr clothing
By dere God I want none
His bonet is of fyne scarlet
With here [hair] as black as geitt [jet]
His dublet ys of fyne satyne
His shertt well mayd and tryme.
His coytt [coat] itt is so tryme and rownde
His kysse is worth a hundred pounde
His hoysse [hose] of London black.
In hyme there ys no lack.

> *Satirical Songs and Poems on Costume* Ed. by F. W. Fairholt

The gown in the late fourteenth and fifteenth century was a fashionable upper garment. It varied in length from reaching the thighs to trailing on the ground (in ceremonial costume). The sleeves were very wide, hanging low down, expanding to a funnel shape below. Others were like hanging pockets and known as bagpipe sleeves. These gowns were worn by both masters and servants and the rank among those serving was marked by the length of their gowns and the sleeves. Domestic servants were notorious for their eagerness to be in the mode and frequently avoided these upper class rules, wearing fashionable gowns however inconvenient. A sarcastic statement on the subject appeared in 1411.

Now have these lords but little need of brooms
To sweep away the filth out of the street,
Since the long sleeves of impecunious grooms
Will lick it up.

> T. Hoccleve *The Regimente of Princes*, ed. F. Furnivall in 1897

Again we have this description of these awkward sleeves:

In the beginning of the king's reign [Richard II] there grew up no little extravagance in Clothes and especially in gowns with deep and wide sleeves called in the vernacular Pokys, like bag pipes in form, so much so that they were used equally by servants and their masters. Which [sleeves] indeed could rightly be called receptacles of devils, since what was furtively taken could be swiftly stowed away in them. Others moreover were so wide and ample that they hung down to the feet, or at least to the knees, full of cuts [ornamental slashes] and bedevilment. Moreover when attendants had to

13. Examples of long funnel-shaped sleeves and bagpipe sleeves. Prince has wide funnel-shaped sleeves so long as to trail on the ground; they are lined with fur. [H]occleve (presenting his book) has bagpipe sleeves, 1410–12.

serve their lords at table with soup, sauces or anything liquid, they at once got immersed in the fluid, tasting it before their masters.

> *Historia Vitae et Regni Ricardi II*
> ascribed to a monk of Evesham, 1390–1399. Trans. from the Latin of Thos. Hearne's edn. of 1729

A curious attitude towards dress developed in the 17th and far more in the 18th century when young men decided periodically to dress like servants, although servants attached to the upper class households were always aping the manners of their masters and mistresses. Orlando in Dekker's play *The Honest Whore* (Part 2) remarks to the Second Servant:

> You proud varlets, you need not be ashamed to wear blue, when your master is one of your fellows.   1630

Here again "blue coat" indicates a serving man or apprentice. R. Holme in his *Academy of Armory* in 1688 also referred to the subject:

> Nay it is a hard thing to distinguish a master from his man, but only that he goes after and stands with his head uncovered before him.

Soame Jenyns was rather shocked by this state of affairs, and in 1756 he wrote expressing his opinion:

> Our very footmen are adorned with gold and silver, toupées and ruffles . . . meanwhile we debase ourselves by a ridiculous imitation of their dresses. Hence are derived the flapped hat, the green frock, the long staff and buck-skin breeches.

and again a little later he said:

The Valet de Chambre cannot be distinguished from his master but by being better dressed.

The World IV (1756)

In 1738 the *London Evening Post* made this commentary:

> There is at present a reigning ambition among our young gentlemen of degrading themselves in apparel to the class of the servants they keep . . . My Lord John wears a plush Frock . . . some had those loose kinds of great-coats which I have heard called 'wrap-rascals' with gold-laced hats slouched in humble imitation of stage-coachmen; others aspired at being grooms . . . .

This apparently grandiose way of life for servants seems to have attracted outsiders, according to Smollett, who wrote:–

> Country folk 'seduced by the appearance of coxcombs in livery . . . swarm up to London in hopes of getting into service where they can live luxuriously and wear fine clothes.

Humphrey Clinker, 1771

It is perhaps not surprising that women servants were even keener than the men to be in the fashion and look smart. The mistress might approve, as long as it enhanced her position in society. A statement in the *Lady's Magazine* of 1785 gives an example of this attitude.

> My wife . . . prides herself on having the smartest servants in the neighbour-hood. Mrs. Becky, . . . does some credit to her taste, who would think she was a *servant* of all work.

Nicholas Udall in his play *Ralph Roister Doister*, 1567, gives us a list

14. A French hood with upper and lower billiments, black streamer hanging behind, 1540.

15. Chambermaid in very fashionable attire, wearing a gown with a stomacher front, short sleeves with embroidered chemise sleeves emerging, her skirt is bustled and her apron without a bib. On her head a fontange-like head-dress, 1700.

of fashionable garments that a servant maid anticipates wearing at her mistress's wedding. These included a French hood with a billiment trimming of gold. The French hood was extremely fashionable at this date and very expensive when trimmed with a billiment of goldsmith's work, which formed an arch round the hood. The maid servant also hoped to wear a "silk cassock . . . fresh and gay" and a farthingale. The feminine cassock was a long loose overcoat. The farthingale, a hooped petticoat, stiff and wide would have been quite unpractical for a maid to work in though possibly she might wear it following a wedding procession.

E

In the 17th century when make up was very fashionable, chamber-maids might have been encouraged by the following statement:

For a penny a chambermaid may buy as much red ochre as will serve seven years for the painting of her cheeks.

H. Peacham *The Worth of a penny* 1641

Hannah Wolley in The *Gentlewoman's Companion* of 1675 advises chamber-maids to

dress well, that you may be able to supply the place of the waiting woman should she chance to be ill.

An extreme example of such smartness is shown in Pl. 7

This urge towards dressing in the fashion was very marked in the eighteenth and nineteenth centuries. An amusing statement by Defoe in *Everybody's Business is Nobody's Business* shows how awkward, at times, it might be.

I was put very much to the blush, being at a friend's House and requir'd of him to salute the Ladies. I kis'd the chamber-jade into the bargain, for she was as well dressed as the best. Things of this kind would be avoided if our Servant Maids were to wear livery as our Footmen do, or if they were obliged to go in a Dress suitable to their station. 1725

Defoe (ibid.) also gives us details of a servant maid's change of clothing in order to be in the fashion.

Her Neats' Leather [ox hide] shoes are now transformed into lac'd shoes with high Heels: her Yarn Stockings are turn'd into fine worsted ones with silk clocks; her high wooden Pattens are kickt away for Leathern Clogs; she must have a Hoop too . . . and her poor scanty Linsey Woolsey [a cloth of linen and wool] petticoat [skirt] is changed into a good silk one 4 or 5 yards wide . . . plain Country Joan is now turned into a fine London Madam.

The clogs at this time were ladies' over-shoes with leather soles and instep straps often very ornamental and matching the elegant shoes. The hoop, an under-petticoat variously distended, was the height of fashion from 1710 to 1780's and would require a skirt of four or five yards wide.

The subject appears to have worried Defoe as he again wrote:

they grow proud and for fear of soiling their gay garments, avoid all manner of household business.

Ibid.

Another writer, in *A Trip through the Town* (Edn. 1735, reprint of Eighteenth Century Tracts, ed. Ralph Straus), echoes the same sentiments.

> Our servant wenches are so puffed up with pride nowadays that they never think they go fine enough. It is a hard matter to know the mistress from the maid by their dress; nay very often, the maid shall be much the finer of the two . . . it seems as if the whole business of the Female Sex were nothing but excess of Pride and extravagance in Dress.

Pl. 6 shows a lady's maid having her hair dressed by the valet. C. P. Moritz in his *Travels in England* 1782, was also impressed by the "force of fashion" in England. He wrote:

> . . . . the poorest servant is careful to be in the fashion, particularly in their hats and bonnets which they all wear.

In *A Present for a Servant Maid*, Eliza Haywood wrote a letter of advice to these maids, warning them not to make the error "of imitating your Betters" and telling them

> . . . . nothing looks so handsome in a servant as a decent Plainness. Ribbands, Ruffles, Necklaces, Fans, Hoop-Petticoats, and all those superfluities in Dress, give you but a tawdry Air and cost you that Money which perhaps you may hereafter have occasion for . . . .

She adds:

> you fear nothing so much as being taken for what you are   1743

On the whole Mrs. Hayward's advice was taken, but those who continued trying to dress above their "station in life" remained the target or critical writers and were always censured by their employers. Even the little maid, Rebecca, in *Mansfield Park* (1814) caused her mistress to be "discomposed" if she saw her going out on Sunday "with a flower in her hat".

The Rev. John Trusler (1735–1820) had very definite views on "dressy servants". He declared that they

> are women of suspicious character and however *genteel* they appear in their own eyes, they are less so in the eyes of others. It is not expected that a young woman should dress herself like an old one; but if she set herself off in her own opinion with fine trumpery or what is called "fal-lal finery" she is only a mark of derision. It is necessary that she should have a sufficient change of underclothes, stockings and pocket handkerchiefs, and outward

useful ones. Indeed, such a wardrobe a prudent mistress will take care to inspect, and take no servant without; otherwise she [the servant] must be ever at the wash-tub.

Domestic Management

The *London Chronicle* of 1791 repeated the same story concerning women servants.

Apeing all the fashions of those they live with . . . mobs to go under the chin are all exploded; silks and muslins and tasty slippers supplant the stiff cotton gowns and strong soaled shoos, formerly used . . . .

However, Sunday seems to have had a sobering influence on some –

When she went out that afternoon to Church, the girl had made herself look something decent and was no longer dressed out as showily as if she was the mistress instead of the maid.

H. & A. Mayhew, *The Greatest Plague of Life*, 1847

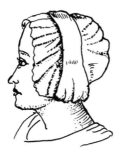

16. A round-eared cap with lappets turned up. Commonly worn by household servants at this time, 1736.

When high waists became the fashion from about 1794–1820 this was a very popular song:

> The servant girls they imitate
> The pride in every place, Sir,
> And if they wear a flower'd gown
> They'll have it made short waist, Sir.
> Printed by J. & M. Robertson, Glasgow, in 1805

Perhaps the most awkward, but correspondingly coveted garment for a maid servant to wear was the hoop petticoat. In 1722 a lady complained of her maid servant from the country, who

had not liv'd with me three weeks before she sew'd three penny canes round the bottom of her shift [chemise] instead of a hoop-petticoat.

Mrs. Centlivre, *The Artifice*

Then again, the nineteenth century hoop-petticoat, the *crinoline*, was very fashionable in the 1850's and 60's. This garment too, was popular with maid servants. See Plate 9 (1863–4). *Punch* of 1863 (XLV, 208) has an amusing skit on the subject.

Mary Did you call Mum?

Lady Yes Mary, I thought I told you not to wear your hoop till you had done your rooms, because you broke the jugs and basins with it!

Mary Oh Mum! You see the Sweeps were coming this morning, and really I couldn't think of opening the door to them with such a figger as I should ha been without my crinoline!

SELF-RESPECT.

Cook (to Fellow-servant who has been after a new Place). "WELL, 'LIZA, WILL IT SUIT?"

Eliza. "NOT IF I KNOWS IT! WHY, WHEN I GOT THERE, BLEST IF THERE WASN'T THE TWO YOUNG LADIES OF THE 'OUSE BOTH A-USIN' OF ONE PIANO AT THE SAME TIME! 'WELL,' THINKS I, 'THIS *HIS* A COMIN' DOWN IN THE WORLD!' SO I THOUGHT I WAS BEST SAY GOOD MORNIN'!"

17. Housemaid, trying to look fashionable, wearing a smart small hat perched on the top of a high chignon at the back of the head. Cook in print dress, small cap and apron, 1874.

18. Housemaid dressed in exaggerated fashion, and wearing a short artificial crinoline, to the surprise of the lady who interviews her, 1860.

In D. Marshall's book "written for the edification of housemaids and parlourmaids" in 1877 we read:

Crinolines are decidedly inconvenient for parlourmaids' and housemaids' work. They cause her to be always in the way. She has no room to pass behind the chairs at table, and she sweeps the ornaments from the tables and what-nots.

A disadvantage for a maid wearing a cheap crinoline was that it tended to collapse in the rain. Surtees in *Plain or Ringlets* 1860 describes the result of a sudden downpour on spectators of a race.

Heavens, what destruction a single minute made of the finery that now distinguishes maid from the mistress! How the artificial flowers were drenched, the gay coquetry taken out of the feathers and the cheap crinoline – the 1s. 11½d. worths reduced to one half their original dimensions.

Then he adds:

> We wonder what our mob-capped grandmothers would say, if they could rise from their graves and see housemaids in hoops.

Breakages were, of course, a hazard, but a real danger was fire. Many casualties resulted from crinolines getting set alight, and for that reason they were forbidden in match factories and others.

In 1863 the *Essex County Standard* wrote:

> We understand that in some of the departments of Messrs. Courtaulds factory, notices have been posted to the effect that fines will for the future be imposed upon those of the gentler sex who shall appear at their work encased in crinolines, which habit, it is put forth, is, in some various occupations, as offensive to decency as dangerous to persons wearing it.

However, crinolines of a sort were sometimes worn by servant girls, possibly to the gratification of "peeping Toms". In a letter of Sir William Hardman concerning fashion in 1863 we read:

> . . . . Crinoline, for example, has it reached its climax?
> Women getting into omnibuses, Servant girls cleaning door steps and virgins at windy seaside watering places, all show their – on occasion.
> *A Mid-Victorian Pepys*, ed. S. M. Ellis, 1923

Bustles in the form of large pads stuffed with wool were in fashion during the 1830's and 40's though the large bustle period was more obvious in the 1880's. However, whenever they were fashionable, maid servants had to wear them. In a latter from Mrs. Carlyle to her mother-in-law in 1834, she describes such a case:

> . . . . The diameter of the fashionable ladies at present is about three yards; their *bustles* are the size of an ordinary sheep's fleece. The very servant-girls wear bustles. Eliza Miles told me a maid of theirs went out one Sunday with three kitchen dusters pinned on as a substitute.
> *Jane Welsh Carlyle,* A New Selection of her Letters,
> arranged by Trudy Bliss

Maids have also been known to use bunched out newspapers for the same purpose.

Was it perhaps possible that a second-hand bustle was not only desired for the sake of fashion, but also because of what it might contain! Had they heard of the old lady who, defrauding the custom-house,

19. Kitchen-maid, aiming at elegance in a décolleté dress, lace trimmed and a lace-edged apron. Shoes with ribbon bows, apron nicely adapted to a bustle, 1890.

.... brought home in her bustle alone ... twelve yards of the best French velvet – upwards of forty-two of Valenciennes lace – a dozen of cambric pocket handkerchiefs – and three dozen of white gloves – nine pair of silk stockings – a pair of stays – and a wig.

H. & A. Mayhew, *The Greatest Plague in Life*, 1847

SUMPTUARY LAWS

Sumptuary Laws, or "Acts of Apparel", which aimed at preventing extravagance, appeared first in Edward IV's reign. These laws applied both to masters and servants, though rather more to servants, whose clothing was largely supplied by their masters.

A Statue concerning diet and apparel, was, however, enacted in 1363:

> Item for the outragious and excessyve apparaile of dyvers people agaynste theyr estate and degree to the greate destruction and impoveryshment of all the lands: It is ordeyned that gromes as well as servauntes of lordes . . . shall . . . have clothes for theyr vesture or hosynge, whereof the hole clothe shall not excede two markes, and that they weare no cloth of higher pryce, . . . nor nothynge of golde nor of sylver, embrowdered [en]aymeled, nor of silver . . . And their wyves, doughters, and children of the same condition in their clothing and apparaile . . . .   (1577 translation)
>   Quoted by W. O. Hassall in *How They Lived*, Vol. I, p. 195

In Queen Elizabeth I's day it was enacted that:

> . . . . it was not lawful for any man [below the rank of a gentelman] either servant or other, to wear their gowns lower than the calves of their legs, except they were above three score years of age.

Gowns, which were over-garments for winter wear, were going out of fashion, but were still worn by servants. An order limiting material used was also made, so that no man under the degree of a knight's eldest son could wear

> velvet in his jerkin, hose or doublet, nor any *satin, damask, taffeta* or *grosgrain* in his clokes, coats, gowns or other uppermost garments.

Sumptuary Laws were also aimed at women servants. In 1481 they were told

> First none shall weare an Ermine or Letis[1] bounet unless shee be a gentle-woman borne hauinge Armes.
>   B.M. MS. Harl. 1776

Again Queen Elizabeth forbade the wearing of "velvet in Kirtles, Peticoats. Sattin in Gowns, Clokes . . . except . . . gentlewomen attendant uppon Countesses, Viscountesses, or ladies of the like or higher

---

[1] A white fur resembling miniver, possibly fur of the snow-weasel.

degree". There were other exceptions, but they do not come under the heading of serving maids.

In the reign of James I, the Common Council of London enacted that servant maids were to wear "no lawn, kambrick, tiffany [a transparent silk gauze] velvet, lawns or white wires on the head or about the kerchief [neck wear] or Koyfe [cap], but only linen and that not to exceed 5s. the ell." Their ruffs were not to be more than four yards in length before being gathered into shape, nor were they to have "any fardingale at all . . . nor any body [bodice] or sleeves of wire, whalebone or other stiffening saving canvas or buckram only". (Quoted by W. Herbert in *Livery Companies of London* 1837.)

At the end of the sixteenth and early seventeenth centuries it was fashionable for sleeves also to be distended, just as were skirts.

SWORDS

The wearing of swords by servants was forbidden by law in 1701; henceforth it was the mark of a gentleman. Previously it was often part of a servant's uniform.

> Where's your blue coat, your sword and buckler, Sir?
> Get you such like habit for a serving-man . . . .
> Henry Porter, *Two Angry Women of Abington*, 1599

Again it was usual for a servant to wear a sword when accompanying his master out walking or shopping. (Plate 8) Pepys wrote in 1662:

> I walked with my wife to my brother Tom's, our boy waiting on us with his sword which this day he begins to wear, to outdo Sir W. Pen's boy, who this day and Sir W. Batten's too, begin to wear new livery. But I do take mine to be the neatest of them all.

In September of the same year he describes the unfortunate results of the fashion for a footman wearing a sword:

> I hear that Captain Ferrers . . . being provoked to strike one of my Lord's footmen, the footman drew his sword and hath almost cut the fingers of one of his hands off . . . .

Among rules of the Charterhouse Hospital in 1622, swords and also gay clothes were frowned upon in households "with standards of humility", and "inferior officers" were forbidden to wear "any weapon . . . [also] long hair, coloured boots, spurs, feathers in their hats or any Russian-like or unseemly Apparel . . ." (Quoted *Notes and Queries* Series V Vol. V 27.)

A satirical account is given, in 1712, by a man who had married a lady "*of Quality*". In place of his old servants she had introduced:

> a couple of Black-a-moors and three or four very genteel Fellows in Laced Liveries, besides her *French*-woman . . . Her footmen . . . are such Beaus that I do not much care for asking them questions . . . She tells me she intends they shall wear Swords with their next Liveries, having lately observed the Footmen of two or three persons of Quality hanging behind the Coach with swords by their sides.
>
> Spectator, No. 299, Feb. 12, 1712

Even as late as 1781 John Crosier wrote:–

> Now so fantastical is the age grown, that its as common to see a puppy at an assembly, perhaps who gets £50 or £60 a year, dress'd in his bag [wig] and *sword* and the next morning you'll see him sweeping his master's doorway and taking down the shutters.
>
> The Diary of John Crosier (unpublished)
The Holly Trees Museum, Colchester

CHAPTER FOUR

Men servants costume of the more outstanding types

UPPER SERVANTS

THE STEWARD like the Controller, Treasurer, Chamberlain, Marshall and Gentleman Usher, followed the fashions of his day, in fact he dressed as an aristocrat. On state occasions the steward was distinguished by wearing a chain of office and carrying a steward's staff. The steward, whose name was "Order" in Philip Massinger's play *A New Way to Pay Old Debts c.* 1630, commands the *usher* thus:

> Set all things right, or as my name is Order
> And by this Staff of office that commands you,
> This chain and double ruff, symbols of power.

Although high ranking servants were dressed like their masters, there appear to have been some rules of etiquette regarding head wear. In medieval days even the marshal, when waiting on his lord, might not wear a head-dress unless it were a coif. The gentleman Usher, if his master were a baron might accompany him out of doors wearing a hat.

> A gentileman husher (but Couered, and not bare-Hedded when he goeth abrode).
>
> B.M. MS. Harl. 1440 f. 14 *A Book of Precedence* (late 16th century)
> ed. F. Furnival, E.E.T.S. Extra Series VIII (1869)

THE PANTER or PANTLER, later BUTLER. He too was dressed according to the style of his day, but like the waiter was instructed to

> Put a towel round your neck for that is courtesy . . . Take the end of the towel in your left hand . . . together with the salt cellar . . . the other end in your right hand with the spoons.   *c.* 1460
>
> John Russell, *Book of Nurture* in *Babees Book*

20. Panter, wearing fashionable long gown with napkin draped round his body ready to serve the meal. Purse suspended from belt, 1485–90.

21. Queen Elizabeth I's butler at a hunting picnic, small apron over his trunk hose. "Then such a place once founde, the Butler first appears", 1575.

22. Butler in tail coat, white waistcoat, breeches and white stockings. "They [the children] were always repulsed by a terrible strong-minded butler who kept guard on the mat and allowed none to pass", 1851.

23. Butler in formal dress clothes which now include trousers instead of breeches, although his master dines alone, 1879.

There appears to have been also a female panter called a *Panetaria* who was mistress of the pantry. Prince Lionel's Household Account books (1356–9) have recorded "a fur-lined bodice" for her. Presumably this was for working in a cold pantry.

As seen in Fig. 21 (1575) the butler wears an apron merely to protect his fashionable clothes while serving out of doors.

After the mid 17th century when livery was no longer worn by high ranking servants, the butler, who was head man, was dressed like his master. A foreigner, coming to England in 1780, found this very confusing and embarrassing. After a visit to the Duke of Newcastle he wrote:

> Ten or twelve servants out of livery attended on us, which would naturally make it difficult for a stranger to distinguish between guests and servants.
> J. W. von Archenholz, *Picture of England*, Trans. in 1791

Even a general manservant might at times dress like his master or wear his master's cast-offs.

The butler's suits, however, were of less expensive material and in the nineteenth century the aim was to have a gentlemanly appearance with

24. Butler behind the scenes in "undress" clothes, wearing a jacket known as a jump. He is in breeches and his cap is in casual style. He carries a bunch of keys, 1665.

an old-fashioned dignity, so that eighteenth century outfits generally continued until about 1870. Breeches, for instance, were still worn when trousers were fashionable. Surtees gives us the picture of a butler in 1831:

> dressed in nankeen shorts, breeches, white gauze silk stockings, white neckcloth, and white waistcoat, with a frill as large as a hand-saw . . . a smart new blue Saxony coat with velvet collar and metal buttons.
>
> See Frontispiece.   *Jorrocks's Jaunts and Jollities*

Soon after 1870, however, there was a drastic change in the correct costume for a butler. It was now contemporary in style, but he wore an evening dress suit, at all times of the day when on duty – a black tail coat, black trousers, white starch-fronted shirt, white waistcoat and white tie.

A butler's 'undress clothes', or other upper servants, in the seventeenth century when off duty or working in the background are shown in Fig. 24 (1665).

They are also described by Surtees in 1831:

> A spruce green gambroon [a cotton mixture] butler's pantry jacket with pockets equal to holding a powder flask each, his lower man being attired in tight drab stocking-net pantaloons [tights] and Hessian boots with large tassels.
>
> *Jorrocks's Jaunts and Jollities*

Hessian boots were popular from the 1790's to 1850's. They were calf-length riding boots and were always decorated with a tassel in front.

A large square-bibbed apron was also a necessary addition to a butler's pantry clothes. One dated 1839 can be seen in the Cardiff Museum. It is made of linen and has neck and waist tapes.

THE CHAMBERLAIN OR VALET

A medieval personal servant is seen dressing his master in Pl. 10 (*c.* 1320). Fig. 25 shows a valet combing his master's hair – (1360). In medieval days he might be the son of a knight and later of a nobleman. Consequently he dressed like his master, whose cast off clothes he often wore. Thomas Dekker in *The Shoemaker's Holiday*, 1600, describes "varlets" at a wedding wearing "buff-jerkins and black gowns": these however were probably servants in general, rather than valets. A

71

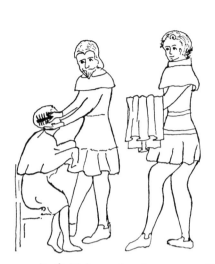

25. (*Left*) Valet and assistant attending on their master (who wears a towel to have his hair combed). They wear fashionable doublets and shoulder capes but no headgear, *c.* 1360.

26. (*Right*) Valet attending the Prince Regent. Both dressed alike in waist-coat and breeches, but the valet still wears a queue wig, 1812.

valet in 1598 is seen in Pl. 8 and another, in the eighteenth century, in Pl. 6 (1772).

Although eventually known as a gentleman's gentleman, the valet could, apparently, at times be a lady's gentleman. Addison, writing in the *Spectator* No. 45, April 1711, said:

> I remember the time when some of our well-bred Country Women kept their Valet de Chambre because, forsooth, a Man was much more handy about them than one of their own Sex. I myself have seen one of these Male Abigails tripping about the Room with a looking glass in his Hand, and combing his Lady's Hair a whole morning together.

In the eighteenth century queue wigs were worn, but a full bottomed must have been rare for a servant. T. Hughes in *Tom Brown's School Days* (1856) states:

> He wore an old full-bottomed wig, the gift of some dandy old Brown whom he had valeted in the middle of the last century.

In the 19th century he was still dressy but tended, like the butler, to remain a little old-fashioned. For example, as in Fig. 26, he could wear a wig in the nineteenth century. Moreover when trousers or pantaloons became correct after *c.* 1815, he continued for a time to wear breeches. See Pl. 12.

THE HERALD

The herald was an important servant in aristocratic families in Medieval and Tudor days, but subsequently he cannot be considered as a private household servant. The garment which he always wore and which distinguished him as a herald was the tabard. It consisted of two rectangular pieces, joined over the shoulders and put on over the head, having a wide neck opening. The panels were sometimes joined at the sides, under the arms, but no belt was worn. A small panel normally overhung each shoulder like an open sleeve or half cape. Shakespeare describes the shape of this garment in *King Henry IV* part 1, IV, ii, 43.

> *Falstaff* There's but a shirt and a half in all my company, and the half shirt is two napkins tacked together and thrown over the shoulders like a herald's coat without sleeves.   1597–8

27. (a) Herald to the King of France in tabard decorated with armorial fleurs de lys, worn over short jacket with long hose and boots with turn-over tops, also spurs, 1485–90. (b) Messenger with an emblematic shield embroidered on his jerkin. He is Sir Pandolph Malatete's herald and is handing a challenge to the Earl of Warwick to a tournament at Vernon, 1485–90.

The tabard was usually very ornamental and embroidered with the arms of the family, initially as a distinguishing label at tournaments. See fig. 27 (1485–90).

THE PAGE

The page, as already mentioned, was, at first, a youth of noble or gentle birth who served in a nobleman's or royal household to receive a training to fit him for his future position in society. Such was the case in the Middle Ages, though after the fifteenth century this practice at Court began to decline, but continued in the households of noble lords up to the end of the 17th century. It is on record that, in 1357, Chaucer himself, at the age of 17, served as a page in the household of Prince Lionel (third son of Edward III) and was supplied with a paltock, a pair of black and red hose, and shoes. The paltock was a type of doublet to which the hose of that period, which were tights (stockings and leg wear all in one) were "trussed", i.e. tied.

In the fifteenth century the cost of various items of livery supplied to "little Edmond Gorges", a page in the Howard household, is re- corded in the *Howard Household Books* (1462–69).

> 1467 a bonet for little Edmonde
> „   peyr shone for Edmon v d.
> „   a seemed gowne for lytelle Edmond xvi d.

(Teenage sons of the house, Thomas and Nicholas Howard, had "seemed gowns" at the same time which cost 2s. each). When Sir J. Howard's wife died in 1465 "Master Edmond Gorges" was supplied with the same mourning attire as were the sons of the house. The fact that little Edmond was sometimes referred to as Master Edmond, implied that he was a gentleman or noble page, and his clothes would be in the fashion of the day, though less expensive.

In the Wardrobe Accounts of Henry VIII, 1535–6, his page Cul- pepir is allowed

> a long gowne of unwatered chamblette . . . furred with conye [rabbit] and lambe.

A long gown would have been a distinction for this page; also he had a black velvet coat lined with purple sarcenet and another of green cloth edged with green velvet. This coat would be synonymous with a jerkin and worn over the doublet. The page was also allowed two doublets, one of black velvet lined with purple sarcenet and another of black satin edged with black velvet, lined with fustian and canvas "all of oure greate wardrobe, for our page aforesaid".

Again the costs of various items supplied to a page in the seventeenth century are listed in the Earl of Bedford's *Household Accounts*:[1]

July 1670	To Mr. Freiston for two periwigs for my lady's page	£2 0s. 0d.
Feb. 1682	For three pair of stockings for Lady Margaret's page	10s. 6d.
	For a hat and case for him	11s. 0d.
	For shoe buckles, buttons for his cuffs and a comb..	3s. 4d.

In March he was allowed 10s. pocket money!

R. Holme in his *Academy of Armory and Blazon* (Book III, Chap. III, p. 70) gives us a description of the garments worn by the page of the Lord Mayor of London in 1688.

.... the Lord Mayor's Page ... his Habit is constant, viz. Doublet and Breeches, Hose and Shooes, all of a colour; with a Loose Coat, or Jacket of scarlet, reaching to the middle of his Thighs, without Sleeves, but such as hang upon his back, being of the same length of his Coat; having a Gold Chain about his Neck, a Velvet Bonnet on his head, with a feather therein: in his left hand he carrieth a White Staff, with a Handkerchief Laced, tied on the top of it, with a poesie of Flowers. In this habit doth a young Boy about 10 to 12 years of age, walk before the Lord Mayor every Easter, etc. when the Aldermen and Sherriffs in their Pomp, wait upon him to the Spittle [Fields].

R. Holme goes on to say that

a Page is in some sence taken to be an office of Servile Imploy ... But Pages in the best acceptation are young Youths of good Birth and Quality, which wait and attend upon Lords and Ladies, Kings and Princes, etc. none under the degree of a Lord having such a person, and by such a Title to attend him: Their Habit is Trunk Breeches ....

In the nineteenth century the page's livery was quite distinctive, so that by his appearance everyone would know that he was a page. He ceased to be of noble birth, but his status was that of an upper servant.

The jacket, sometimes called a tunic, was short to the waist and closed

---

[1] Quoted in M. Harrison and O. Royston, *How They Lived, 1685–1700.*

28. The Lord Mayor's elegant page in his doublet and breeches, with the sleeveless jerkin, showing the hanging sleeves. On his head the velvet feather-trimmed "bonnet", 1688.

29. Page, in correct livery, short jacket with stand collar, trousers with white stripe down the outside of leg. "Who would be a page?", 1858.

all down the front, so that no waistcoat was worn. This jacket, somewhat military in style, often had shoulder bands, like a soldier's, but
here they were used to hold the page's gloves. His leg wear was pantaloons, i.e. tights, or sometimes long trousers, blue with a red stripe
down the sides. Out of doors he wore a top hat with side strings from
brim to crown. See Plates 10 and 25. From about 1890 a pill-box cap
replaced the top hat. An amusing description in 1847 was given by a
lawyer's wife engaging an orphan boy as a page:

> The jacket was a claret, with three rows of sugarloaf buttons as close
> together as a rope of onions . . . pair of nice quiet dark coloured pantaloons
> running rather into the port wine than partaking of the claret . . . and to
> guard against the brat's growing out of them before they were fairly worn
> out, I had taken the wise precaution of having three tucks put in at the
> bottom of them.
> In not less than a week it "was not fit to be seen".
> H. & A. Mayhew, *The Greatest Plague in Life*

30. Page in top hat and coat with three rows
of buttons, 1889.

The custom of arranging on the padded chest of the page's jacket one, two or even three rows of buttons, with as many as eighteen in each row, gave him the popular name of "Buttons". Thackeray refers to these buttons in *The Book of Snobs* 1846

> Thomas or Tummus works in the garden or about the pigstye and stable; Thomas wears a page's costume of eruptive buttons.

31. Page in dark green livery, "with a lace sham-hole on the collar". It buttons up to the neck and has a pointed cuff and thirty brass buttons – for a boy of 14, 1894.

On ceremonial occasions, breeches instead of pantaloons were worn. This is Creevey's description of a page (his own nephew) who was to attend King William IV's coronation in 1831.

> A scarlet tunic with standing collar and black stock, no waistcoat, white breeches and silk stockings, gilt buckles both knees and shoes, and a blue sash.

> *Creevey's Life and Times*, ed. John Gore

Joseph Couts, in his *Practical Guide for the Tailor's Cutting Room*, 1848, states:

> The jacket for a page should be cut like a military jacket. The ornaments such as buttons, braiding, cuffs, flaps, collar, etc., etc., all depend upon the heraldic or other rule of the family to which he belongs. The trousers for a page must be cut like those for any other youth of a similar size and age.

32. Page, showing back view of his jacket. He wears trousers with the usual stripe. Footman in tail coat and breeches, 1892.

LOWER RANKS

THE FOOTMAN

When waiting at table and when accompanying his master or attending to guests, a footman would always wear livery. In style his clothing would conform to the fashion of the day, however inconvenient for his work.

There might, however, be some modifications, as in the sixteenth century when trunk hose were the mode (from *c.* 1550–1670). This leg wear consisted of a widely distended upper portion from the waist all round the seat and joined to the stocking portion near the fork. Servants were not often allowed to be so puffed out unless attending royalty. (See Queen Elizabeth's groom.) When in the 1570's, for ordinary wear, trunk hose were discarded for breeches, these latter became the footman's leg wear to the end of the nineteenth century (and on).

When not on duty informal clothes were allowed, such as: "the footman's undress jacket of linen", 1461 (Contemporary account quoted in *Domestic Life in England* by the editor of the *Family Manual*, 1835.)

In the Privy Purse Expenses in 1503 of Elizabeth of York, Queen of Henry VII (ed. Sir N. H. Nicolas 1830), we find:

> Item for making of thre dublettes of satyn of Bruges for the Quenes fotemen at xxd the pece vs. Item for making of iii jakettes of blake velvet lyned with sarcenet for the same fotemen at xijd. the pece iijs.

The jackets, later known as jerkins, were worn over the doublets.

In the early sixteenth century, the Earl of Northumberland, when anticipating a voyage overseas, arranged for his footmen to have

> ii dowbletts of grene satten . . . iiii dowbletts of sattyn of briguse . . . two dowbletts of yellow, and ii of orrenge collar tawney. ii paire of gardit[1] hose of rede and blake cloth for the said ii foutmen.
>
> *Earl of Northumberland Household Book, 1512–25*
> F. Grose, *Antiquarian Repertory*, Vol. 4

In the eighteenth century the footman's livery still followed the fashions of his day, changing little until the late nineteenth century. It consisted of a collarless knee-length coat, worn open or merely buttoned at the top, a long waistcoat and knee breeches, often made of plush, white silk stockings and buckled shoes or indoor pumps. See Pls. 13(d), 14 and 15. After the 1730's his coat usually had a turn-down collar, a less formal style known as a frock – (no relation to the frock coat). The collar and cuffs would have a contrasting colour. His coat would be decorated with his "trade-mark", the outmoded "shoulder knot", sometimes tipped with ornamental metal tags called aiglets. See Pl. 14 (1812). His buttons would be stamped with his employer's crest instead of his having it embroidered on his coat. A Birmingham manufacturer was said to have a selection of 10,000 dies ready for stamping these buttons when required.

Out of doors the great coat or "surtout" fell below the knees. It followed the line of the "frock" but the front skirt was not sloped away from mid-line. It was made with a curious vestigial remains, the

---

[1] Particoloured and old-fashioned.

sword-slash, a slit in the side seam under the arm and having a "flap" inside to cover the gap. Through this the footman could reach his non-existent sword. Instead of a sword he might carry a tall cane, often silver or gold headed. The cane was a distinctive feature of a footman's livery. To quote from G. Farquhar's play *The Beaux Stratagem* 1707, in reply to "What sort of livery has the footman?" the servant exclaims:

> Livery! Lord Madam, I took him for a captain, he's so bedizened with lace and then he has . . . a silver-headed cane dangling at his knuckles . . . and has a fine long periwig tied up in a bag.

The bag wig in which the queue was enclosed in a square black silk bag drawn in at the nape of the neck by a running string concealed by a stiff black bow, was worn with "dress" and "full dress" in the eighteenth century by gentlemen.

As regards the footman's hair styles, the wig, so universally worn by gentlemen, continued to be correct for footmen all through the century. See Fig. 41 (1848). In the very early years some masters objected to wigs, but the hair had to be powdered.

> there's nothing we Beaux take more pride in than a sett of Genteel Footmen. I never have any but what wear their own Hair, and I allow 'em a Crown a week for Gloves and Powder.
>
> *Tunbridge Walks*, 1703

In varying styles and quality, wigs were the head wear of men all through the eighteenth century, despite their inconvenience for work. P. Kalm, the Frenchman, on his visit to England in 1748 wrote:

> Men all wore them [wigs] from servants, clod-hoppers, day labourers . . . in a word all labouring folk go thro' their everyday duties all with perukes on their heads. Pl. 14   (1812).

The footman's outdoor head wear was a "bicorne" or "tricorne" cocked hat often trimmed with gold "lace", i.e. braid, and sometimes with a cockade. (See Fig. 33 and Pl. 16.)

Susan Sibbald, describing school life in Bath in 1797, was obviously thrilled by the appearance of the footmen.

> Then up came livery servants, none with a smarter livery than Thomas, Mrs. Gambier's footman, cockade in his hat and tall cane. He touched his hat . . . away I went passing the girls with the smartest footman behind me and I dare say feeling proud.
>
> People were not very strict on Sundays in those days, so Mrs. G. took me

33. A peer's footman waits at the rear of the carriage while the ladies shop.
He wears a green coat with brick-red cuffs, plum-red breeches; epaulettes and
all lacing gold. Black bicorne hat with cockade, white stockings with black
clocks, buckled shoes, 1808.

with her to make sundry calls. The footmen accompanied their mistresses
to knock at the doors and then stood outside. Sometimes there were three
or four at one time together. If you saw the livery of anyone you did not
like, you would pass on.

The Memoirs of Susan Sibbald, 1783–1812
ed. Francis P. Hett, her great-grandson

An American, describing what he saw at a Royal birthday soon after
1800, was equally impressed.

The livery of the footmen was also gaudy and fantastical to the last degree.
They wore lace [braid] not only on the borders, but on all the seams of
their garments, and their large cocked hats were surrounded with broad
fringes of silver or gold. On such occasions as these it is a point of great
ambition to display the finest equipage.

An Equipage in England described by an American,
Sussex Archeological Collection, XV

Protective clothing was required and often supplied for footmen when
employed on menial work. Henry Purefoy wrote in 1747 to his tailor:

Bring 3 Linnen washing frocks for 3 menservants who were footmen, such
as you used to bring; let them be big enough, the last were too tite upon 'em.
Purefoy Letters, 1735–53, Vol. II, p. 321

In 1734 a gentleman bought a "white frock" for one of his footmen
"to powder my periwigs in". (FitzWalter's Account Book, Essex
Record Office.) And the Duke of Bedford supplied every footman for
rough work, with coarse shirts, leather or cloth breeches, worsted
stockings and heavy shoes.

Here is a footman's description of his "menial work":–

> I'll try to tell in easy Rhyme
> How I in London spend my time . . .
> I rise from Bed and down I set me
> To cleaning glasses, knives and Plate
> And such like dirty Work . . .
> This done; with expeditious care
> To dress myself I strait prepare;
> I clean my Buckles, black my Shoes
> Powder my Wig, and brush my Cloaths;
> Take off my Beard, and wash my Face,
> And then I'm ready for the Chase.   1732

An Epistle to my friend Mrs. Wright *The Footman's Miscellany*

In the nineteenth century the footman's outfit persisted in the eighteenth century styles and many continued to the end of the century to have a tailcoat worn open, knee breeches, white stockings and, indoors, slippers called pumps, which had short uppers. See Pl. 15 (indoor livery) Plate 16 (outdoor).

A red tasselled cord dangling from the left shoulder, known as the "flash string" (corruption of "flask string") was the special badge of the attendants of Royalty when travelling. It was merely decorative, though originally made to suspend a flask of gunpowder. The shoulder knot was worn with full dress livery.

Surtees frequently describes footmen, and in *Ask Mama*, 1850, we find, at Tantivy Castle the abode of an earl, this account:

> There are always at least half a dozen powdered *footmen* in cerulean blue lined with rose-coloured silk, and pink silk stockings, the whole profusely illustrated with *gold lace, gold aiglets*[1] and I don't know what, lounging about in the halls and passages.

The pink silk stockings were unusual, white having become established as correct for a footman. It was, alas for him, a favourite trick of street urchins to splash these stockings with mud, just as they would stick pins into his calves, when he was stationary, to see if they were real or stuffed. Footmen with thin legs often had to wear false calves which were pads worn inside their stockings to improve the shape of their legs.

From the 1850's a footman's less formal wear, especially when sitting beside the coachman on the box, was a *coatee*. This was a shortened dress coat, ending about 2 inches above the knee. It had a sword slash and many buttons, such as:

> Buttons plain gilt or plated with family crest. Invariably made up with 50 buttons up the front, slashes on skirts with 3 buttons, 3 buttons in pleats and sleeve cuff with 2 buttons.
>
> *The West End Gazette of Fashion*, Feb. 1865

But the arrangement of buttons varied. Surtees mentions the coatee in 1854 and once again pink stockings:

> Out rush the powdered flunkeys in red plush breeches, pink silk stockings and blue coatees.
>
> *Handley Cross*

---

[1] Ornamental metal tags tipping the shoulder knot.

34. (*Left*) Footman's full dress livery with shoulder knot. Note his horizontally striped waistcoat, 1894.

35. (*Right*) Footman's coatee, front and back, as described in text. Note the horizontally striped waistcoat, 1894.

The footman's waistcoat deserves special mention as it was often striped. See Pl. 15(a). The convention was that the stripes should be horizontal for indoor servants and vertical for outdoor. Surtees[1] pokes fun at a country footman whose stripes were vertical, which was correct only for outdoor wear. White Berlin gloves, made of a kind of strong cotton, "thin, neat and washable" were worn indoors and out.

From about mid-nineteenth century a well dressed footman might wear trousers; in fact he wore the evening dress suit of a gentleman, even to a white bow tie in the evening (Fig. 36) (1892). The only difference was that his coat had decorative brass buttons, most of them

[1] Jorrocks's *Jorrocks's Jaunts and Jollities.*

36. Footman in the evening dress of a gentleman even to a white bow tie, 1892.

being functionless, but representing "the insignia of servitude". Fig. 37 (1880). The undress livery of a footman in 1871 was described thus:

> Double-breasted coat, 6 button holes in lapels . . . sleeves with plain cuff, having one button above the top and one button below. Skirt short . . . with a pointed sword slash and 3 large buttons on it . . . .
> Vest single-breasted with roll collar of striped Valencia . . . .
> Trousers straight with whole falls front.
> > *The Sartor or British Journal of Cutting, Clothing and Fashion*
> > Vol. iii, Nov. 1871–April 1872

A footman's protective clothing when he was cleaning knives or doing similar jobs, comprised

> An overall, a waistcoat, a fustian jacket and a leather apron, with a white apron to put on occasionally when called from these duties.
> > S. & S. Adams, *The Complete Servant*, 1825

37. (*Left*) Young footman in coatee and trousers *c.* 1880.
38. (*Centre*) Footman's pantry suit, 1894.
39. (*Right*) Footman's Box Coat. "Total length about 54 inches", 1894.

It was usual for a man servant to wear livery when he was acting as a footman, but if he had to undertake other jobs it was awkward:

> Having to act the part of groom and gamekeeper during the morning, and butler and footman in the afternoon, he was attired in a sort of composition dress, savouring of the different characters performed. He had
> an old white hat
> a groom's fustian stable-coat cut down into
> a shooting jacket with a whistle at the button hole
> red plush smalls and top boots.
> R. S. Surtees, *Jorrocks's Jaunts and Jollities,* 1831–4

The footman's pantry suit, towards the end of the nineteenth century, was a short jacket, striped waistcoat and trousers. Fig. 38 (1894). To quote from T. H. Holding, the pantry suit was called a Jean jacket and striped waistcoat which is worn for work in the pantry and about the house, but a servant does not, except by special permission, enter any of the rooms on service thus clad . . . .

The jacket is made 23 inches long . . . is worn over the striped evening vest.

British Uniforms, 1894

Out of doors long overcoats, reaching down to the feet, were correct for head footmen during the second half of the nineteenth century.

Footman's great coat is very long, pockets in pleats. Never has flaps and side pockets, seams are plain.

The West End Gazette of Fashion, Feb. 1877

(A specimen five feet long can be seen at the London Museum.) When not encumbered with these they might still carry a long cane. For example:

40. Footman in attendance, wearing tailcoat, short waistcoat, top hat with cockade and holding a cane, also carrying the ladies' books, 1859.

Tim . . . followed me and my mother to church, carrying a huge prayer-book and a cane, and dressed in the livery of one of our own footmen . . . .
Thackeray *Barry Lyndon*, 1844

Again Surtees refers to these canes in *Handley Cross*, 1854:
The butler shouts

"Missis coming down!" whereupon the Johnnies rush to their silver-laced hats on the hall table, seize their gold-headed canes, pull their white Berlins out of their pockets and take a position on each side of the barouche door.

He also describes what a footman might wear out of doors without any overcoat.

A footman's morning jacket – resembling the coatee – of dark grey cloth with a stand-up collar, plentifully besprinkled with large brass buttons with raised edges, waistcoat of broad blue and white stripes made up stripe length ways, baggy pair of blue plush shorts, tight drab gaiters with Berlin gloves.

Gaiters were sometimes a footman's leg wear. On his feet the footman wore buckled shoes out of doors.

Snuff-coloured coat and vest, claret-coloured shorts, buckled shoes and large double-jointed brass-headed cane.
R. S. Surtees, *Ask Mamma*, 1858

Hair styles: Powdered hair or wigs were still worn by footmen well into the nineteenth century and long after they had gone completely out of fashion. The wigs worn were usually tie wigs, wigs with a queue or sometimes bag wigs.

When the footman's wig was at last given up, in accordance with the English habit of clinging to tradition with symbols of the past, the great coat was sometimes decorated with a "bag" which was a black bow or tab placed at the back of the neck representing the non-existent bag wig. See Fig. 42.

When footman no longer wore wigs, their own hair often had to be powdered:

A quantity of flour concealed the natural colour of his wild matted hair.
R. S. Surtees, *Handley Cross*, 1854

Head wear out of doors continued as in the eighteenth century, the cocked hat being correct for dress wear. After 1830, however, the silk top hat replaced it for undress wear. Pl. 16 (1848). If the master was in

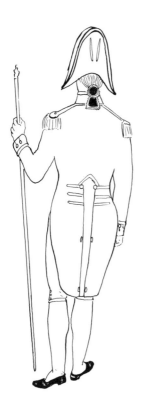

41. Footman in maroon tailcoat with gold braid and epaulettes, white breeches and stockings, his bicorne hat laced with gold; garters gold and shoes black. He wears a modified bag wig with black ribbon edged with gold and carries a long staff, 1848.

43. (Facing) Small footman in jacket, trousers and large top hat, 1849.

42. Footmen of a Magnate. They wear symbolic black bows at the back of the neck representing the now extinct bag wig. 1880.

WHO WOULDN'T KEEP A FOOTMAN!

43.

any office under the crown, the hat might be decorated with a black Hanoverian cockade, or at a wedding with a white one. The cockade was placed on the left side of the top hat. See Fig. 40 (1859) and Pl. 1(a).

THE APPRENTICE

The apprentice from Elizabethan days to the eighteenth century was a household servant of lower rank, working for his master while learning a trade. He was therefore a servant whose stay was limited. The Frenchman, Misson, wrote in his *Mélanges sur l'Angleterre* in 1784:

> Before a servant can enter a house, he must have served his apprenticeship. Parliament has enacted that he must live for six years with an employer who will not pay him wages, but will clothe him and feed him.
>
> (Translation by S. C. Roberts)

In Elizabethan days the apprentice was often a gentleman, but his clothing, although conforming to a style of the day, was severely restricted on economical grounds. A gentleman's doublet was padded in front, his was not. His breeches were "small plain slops". Slops were wide baggy breeches closed at the knee and were unfashionable country wear. He was not supposed to wear silk stockings, ruffs or hand ruffs and his head wear was a woollen cap. The materials for his clothes were canvas, leather, sackcloth or fustian and the colours had to be sober, such as russet or sometimes blue.

(M. St. Clare Byrne *Elizabethan Life in Town and Country*, 1961.)

In the eighteenth century the apprentices' "greasy woollen Night-Caps" were often referred to, for example in *Trips through the Town* 1735 edn. and again Misson had this to say:

> An apprentice is a sort of a slave; he wears neither Hat nor Cap in his Master's presence; he cant marry nor have any Dealings on his own Account.
>
> *Ibid.*

Actually the apprentice might wear his cap in his master's presence during the last year of his time.

MEN SERVING AT TABLE

From the eleventh to the fourteenth century men serving at table, including cup bearers, usually wore a short tunic and, as a rule, had a napkin, often draped round the neck (Pl. 22(a)), or over the arm. In the Bayeux Tapestry a servant on bended knee is thus depicted. He holds a bowl near the table of William the Conqueror. The serving man's napkin was used instead of a glove for cleanliness when holding a dish

44. Pilate washing his hands, attended by a "sewer" with a towel round his neck. He wears a short tunic and a coif on his head, 1280.

45. Cup bearer (on right) in short belted tunic holding a bowl with a napkin.
Bare headed. In front of him is "Lot entertaining angels unawares". Eleventh
century.

46. Server in long tunic and holding a napkin in left hand, a flask in right. He
is bare headed. Eleventh century.

or a cup, as in Pl. 17. It is not to be confused with the towel offered for hand washing before a meal (Cf. Fig. 44).

Although these medieval servants were generally menials, in some cases a high-ranking servant might act as waiter, in which case his tunic, or in the fifteenth century his gown, would be long. Compare Fig. 46 and Fig. 20.

A later example of the use of a napkin is seen in Turberville's *Book of Hunting* 1575 where a picnic scene is illustrated. A gentleman carries one as he hands a goblet to Queen Elizabeth, as has always been the rule for men serving at table. This cupbearer, even though out of doors, is bare-headed.

INDOOR GROOMS also served at meals.

One rule which had to be obeyed was:

No groom's head to be covered serving at meals,
yemen ne yeman Jentilmen ne Jentilmen the Steward.
A 15th-century Courtesy Book ed. R. W. Chambers, 1914

Henry VIII provided "fyve cootys of grene clothe styched with grene silke, having buttons of like silke . . . for fyve groomes of oure preavie chambre" in 1535. (*Archaeologia* Vol. 9, Henry VIII's Wardrobe Account.)

When acting as waiters in Charles II's reign, the following order was laid down:

Grooms[1] of the Privy-Chamber in Ordinary in number 6, all gentlemen of Quality these [as all grooms] wait without sword, cloak or hat: whereas the Gentlemen wear alwayes cloak and sword.
Anglicae Notitia or *The Present State of England*
Edward Chamberlayne. John Martyn 1st ed. 1669

From the seventeenth century on, the groom was an outdoor servant in charge of horses (see p. 109).

THE HENCHMAN was an attendant with very varied duties – a humble messenger by the fifteenth century.

In the Household Accounts of Sir John Howard we are told that in 1463 he was sent to ride to London and the same year to Colchester "ffo to schoe my mastterys hors" for which he was given some money and "a peyre of hoseys" and the garments he received from 1463 to 1467

[1] Gentlemen in Ordinary.

47. Young boy server wearing a short doublet, breeches and having long hair. Unlike the family, who wear hats although at table, he is bareheaded, 1665.

were a doublet, two shirts, boots, shoes, a jacket, "pynsons" [indoor shoes] and a "short gowne of blak . . . russett fryse to the same . . . of vyolett . . . and blak lynynge". (*Manners and Household Expenses . . .* ed. B. Botfield, Roxburghe Club, 1841.)

The henchman ceased to function as a household servant from the seventeenth century.

THE FOOL was a favoured servant, pampered, and generally presented with elegant clothing.

Henry VIII in 1535–6 provided his fool with a doublet of worsted lined with canvas and cotton, also a coat and a cap of green cloth fringed with red crewel,[1] and a coat of green cloth with a hood which had a fringe of white crewel and another coat with a fringe of red and white crewel and lined with buckram. (Excerpt from a MS. transcribed by John Caley in *Archaeologia* Vol. 9.)

Thomas Coryat in his *Crudities* 1611, refers to

a Whitsuntide foole, disguised like a foole wearing a long coate.

[1] Crewel was a two-threaded worsted, used chiefly for garters, girdles and trimmings, especially of the lower classes.

The Lestrange Household Accounts (1519–78) record that their fool, in 1520, was provided with:

iii yerds of blankett for a petycote and a payr of slopps [Loose breeches].

The man's petticoat at this date was an under-doublet worn for warmth.

In wynter next your shirt use you to wear a pettycott of scarlet.
Andrew Boorde, *Dyetary of Helth* (1542)
ed. F. J. Furnival, E.E.T.S. E.S.X.

Queen Elizabeth's black fool was well provided with a gay wardrobe of clothes, made to measure. He had a velvet coat, corresponding to a jerkin, which was decorated with "panes", long slashes, producing red, green and yellow stripes. He was given a striped doublet with silk buttons and bombasted, i.e. padded out in front, in the height of fashion. He had several pairs of "gascons", wide breeches, with the close fitting extensions called "canions" and many elegant stockings and silk garters. Also

Item for one colored felte [hat] for the said blak-a-more, trymed with taphata, layed with lase with a Rolle of red and yellowe sipers [a silk and linen mixture]...a hatt of tapheta garnished with lase of sundry colors with fether of colors with golde spangells to it.

In addition to all this he was provided with "two cases for his Instruments". We are not told what they were! (1575, B. M. Egerton 2806 f. 84).

Queen Elizabeth also kept some women dwarfs for her entertainment. They too were provided with gay apparel, such as "two gownes the one white damaske, thother blewe chamblett...layed wth copper lase lyned with fustian and rolles of cotton in the pleites..." This would help to give the effect of wearing the fashionable farthingale to distend the skirt. One woman dwarf had "fouer Cawles [head wear] of...golde and silver: thre netteworke parteletts" [a fill-in, for a low décolletage]. (1578 B.M. MS. Egerton 2806 f. 112, 123, 131.)

MALE COOKS

In the Middle Ages cooks dressed according to the style of the day, but without any overgarment, because of the heat. Their distinguishing mark was an apron, a garment rarely worn by men at this time. Pls.

19(a), 20. In the fifteenth century illustrations of the *Canterbury Tales*[1] the cook wears a long white apron even on horse back. Pl. 18.)

In the seventeenth and eighteenth centuries, as a protection from being splashed with hot liquids, he might wear long white oversleeves. (Pl. 21.)

> Cooke with cap, sleeves and apron.
>
> R. Holme, *Academy of Armory*, 1688

In the 18th century cooks usually wore a round skull cap of velvet or white linen, which was known as a "night cap" though for day wear! This night cap would probably cover a bald head, since when not on duty the cook would wear a wig, so universally worn by most men in this century.

In the nineteenth century the cook was usually a woman, for ordinary households.

> In England men cooks are kept only in about 300–400 great wealthy families . . . The man cook in the establishment of a man of fashion is generally foreign, in fact a chef.
>
> S. &. S. Adams, *The Complete Servant*, 1825

The male cook, however, continued with his apron, but his headgear varied. At first he wore a stiff white toque. The stiffening remained, but the shape underwent various transformations in cut. In 1843 they wore round flat-topped tam-o-shanters or sometimes a peaked cap. Soon after a pointed "dunce's" cap might be seen, a skull cap or a "pork-pie" with a tassel.

Thackeray describes a fashionable chef in 1852 as:

> sporting a rich crimson velvet waistcoat . . . a variegated blue satin stock . . . and a white hat worn on one side of his long curling ringlets.
>
> *A Little Dinner at Timmins's*

In 1892 the cook's hat, for the first time, was cylindrical and a little taller than the pork pie, but the modern cook's hat, tall starched and white, belongs to the next century and does not appear to have been worn by cooks employed as household servants before this.

---

[1] Ellesmere Chaucer in Facsimile (Manchester University Press) 1911.

48. Cook wearing an apron. Coat cream-coloured, waistcoat blue, breeches green, untidy stockings bluish and wrinkled. He wears a cook's white starched cap. A contrast between him and the liveried footman's attire, 1808.

THE CARVER

The carver, as a household servant belongs to the Middle Ages. (Pl. 22(b).) Like the cook, he wore an apron unless he was honorary carver of the King. There was also

> a general Rule to every gentilman that is Kerver to any maner Lorde. A towel muste be layed vppon his shoulder when he shall bryng his lorde brede.
>
> *A Fifteenth Century Courtesy Book*
> ed. R. W. Chambers, E.E.T.S. orig. ser. 148 (1914)

KITCHEN BOYS

These youths, who worked for the kitchen staff, were provided with clothes, certainly to the end of the 16th century. The Lestrange Accounts give a number of items given to kitchen boys between 1520 and 1530. "The boye of the Kechyn" was supplied with a canvas shirt,

49. Cook at school, throwing pancakes. He wears a white jacket, a long apron and a pointed cook's cap, 1863 (see text).

a coat, a loose fitting jacket, worn as an overgarment, a doublet and "blancket[1] to make ye boye of ye kechyn a payer of hose". (*Archaeologia* XXV.) He also had leather shoes.

THE SCULLION

This man doing the dirty work of the kitchen from the Middle Ages well into the seventeenth century, seems to have been clothed in dirt himself. There appears to be evidence that Henry VIII's kitchen scullion lay about filthy and tattered or even naked. This became so scandalous that the King issued orders that

> the three master cookes shall have . . . yearly twenty marks to the intent they shall provide and sufficiently furnish the said kitchens of such scolyons as shall not goe naked or in garments of such vilenesse as they now doe.
> Quoted in *Medieval Man and his Notions*
> by Frederick Harrison, Canon Chancellor & Librarian of York Minster
> [J. Murray, London, 1947]

In our picture of a scullion (Pl. 23) in *c.* 1686, the coat is patched and shabby. He was, however, a famous character for apart from his kitchen duties, he is said to have been employed to sing satirical and political ballads against the party of James II previous to the revolution of 1688.

OUTDOOR SERVANTS

THE RUNNING FOOTMAN

A running footman who, as already described, had to run in front of his master's coach, would need clothing that was light in weight and also colour; something that would show up when the coach was travelling after dark. Therefore white was usual.

These men functioned mainly in the seventeenth and eighteenth centuries and sometimes in the nineteenth; but in their appearance they had something in common with the earlier footman who ran beside his master on horseback.

In the sixteenth century Lord Northumberland's footmen had

> ii p'e of playn white hosse . . . to ryne [run] in.

---

[1] A white woollen cloth used by the humbler classes.

and they were also provided with

> ii long arrowes like standarts with socetts of stell to carry in their hands when the ryn with my Lorde.[1]

Sir Thomas Overbury describes him in the following way.

> Let him be never so well made, yet his Legs are not matches: for he is still setting the best foot forward . . . Hee is very long winded: and, without doubt, but that he hates naturally to serve on horsebacke, hee had proved an excellent trumpet. Hee has one happiness above all the rest of the Servingmen, for when he most overreaches his Master, hee's best thought of. Hee lives more by his owne heat then the warmth of his clothes – and the waiting-woman hath the greatest fancy to him when he is in his close trous. Gardes hee weares none: which makes him live more upright then any cross gartered gentleman-usher.
>
> Sir Thomas Overbury, The Overburian Characters, 1615
Ed. by W. J. Paylor, B.A., B.Litt.

The following is a description of the running footman's apparel by Randle Holme in *Academy of Armory* 1688.

> He was generally for ease of speedy going clothed in light thin cloaths, all in white, as doublet, slashed or open, breeches or drawers, and stockings of the same, thin soled shoes called "pumps". These men run by their Lord's coach or horse's side.
>
> T. Middleton, A Mad World My Masters, 1608

A nickname for a running footman in the seventeenth century was "Linnen stocks and threescore miles a day". T. Middleton, *A Mad World My Masters*, 1608.

However, the footman, known as the "running footman" featured chiefly in the eighteenth century. Some of them retained a court fashion of the later seventeenth century, for their leg wear, and this was petticoat breeches. These resembled a divided skirt, being immensely wide in the leg, gathered into a waistband and falling to the knees or just above. They must have been very convenient for running in when knee breeches tended to be close-fitting. These petticoat breeches were sometimes weighted by a deep gold fringe, when worn without drawers, supposedly for decency's sake, but not always. We are told that:

---

[1] *Antiquarian Repertory*, Vol. 4.

Village Maids delight to see
Running Footmen fly bare-ars'd
O'er the dusty road.   1725
Quoted by C. Bovill in *English Country Life*, 1963

Drawers were more usual, worn under the petticoat breeches. The *Gentleman's Magazine* of 1726 sums up his costume thus:

Drawers, stockings, pumps, cap, sash and petticoat-breeches.

The *Weekly Journal* of 1730 gives more details.

Fine Holland drawers and waistcoat, thread stockings, a blue silk sash fringed with silver, a velvet cap with a great tassel; and carry a porter's staff with a large silver handle.

These running footmen always carried long staves, with a ball on the head, possibly for use as a container.

The running footmen drank white wine and eggs. One told me, fifty years ago that they carried some white wine in the large silver ball of the tall cane, or pole which unscrews.
Quoted by Rev. George Ashby, in 1780
Notes and Queries, 2nd series (1856) 19

Scott also refers to them in *The Bride of Lammermoor*, 1819.

Two running footmen, dressed in white with black jockey-caps and long staffs in their hands, headed the train; and such was their agility that they found no difficulty in keeping the necessary advance which the etiquette of their station required before the carriage and horsemen.

There is a public house in Charles Street, Berkeley Square, called "The Running Footman" which had as its sign a picture captioned "I am the only Running Footman" of which Chambers' *Book of Days* (1863–4) gives a description:

A light black cap, a jockey coat, white linen trousers [in the illustration he wears breeches] or a mere linen shirt coming to the knees, with a pole six or seven feet long . . . On the top of the pole was a hollow ball in which he kept a hard boiled egg, or a little white wine to serve as a refreshment on the journey.

It is said that the Duke of Queensberry, who died in 1810, continued to employ a running footman longer than any other of the London grandees.

50. The character "Teague", wearing the livery typical of a Running Footman: blue coat with silver lacing, petticoat breeches with silver fringe and
blue sash. His black velvet cap is worn by the drunken Puritan (an exchange
of hats for fun). When offered employment Teague had said: "I will run for
thee forty miles, but I scorn to have a trade." 1775

H

THE COACHMAN

As with other liveried servants, the coachman's colours would be his master's choice and his garments according to the contemporary style. (See Pl. 13(b).) However, because of his association with horses, he always wore breeches, and on the box, jack boots or gaiters. The following letter shows how important it was for a coachman to be dressed correctly for the family he served.

> July 10th, 1743.
> I desire you will make the coachman a ffrock the same coloured cloath to the pattern as near as you can and a gold coloured serge paduasoy waist-coat. Pray let the serge paduasoy be better than the last was. It must not be lemon colour, but a gold colour, and the lining of the frock must be of the same colour; . . . and hee shall wear . . . a pair of boots.
> *Purefoy Letters*, Vol. II, ed. G. Eland

From the late eighteenth century, throughout the nineteenth, when driving in bad weather, he generally wore a heavy caped overcoat, (see Pl. 24), the capes often multiple. It was known as a box coat. A tricorne hat was usual in the eighteenth century; subsequently the top hat was correct. See Pl. 29. The hat might be decorated with feathers. The *Morning Post* in 1777 made this comment:

> Lord Derby's coachman and footman with their red feathers, and flame-coloured silk stockings, looked like so many figurantes, taken from behind the scenes of the opera house.

Protective clothing for rough work is prescribed in 1746, in another of the Purefoy Letters (Vol. II):

> I desire you will bring . . . the Coachman a linnen frock to put over his cloaths when he rubs his horses down.   1746
> Vol. II

In the nineteenth century the coachman wore a frock coat, "whilst for stable wear and ordinary purposes, they have the choice of either the no-collar or step collar finish at the neck" (Vincent's *Cutter's Practical Guide* 1890–5).

The livery waistcoat, or vest, of a coachman was usually long and finished over the hips with a slit at the side seam and buttoned high. If stripes were present, these would be vertical for both a coachman and a groom, since they were outdoor staff. The vest was sometimes made of the same material as the coat or sometimes a self-coloured Cassimere of bright colour, such as red, or it may be a striped Velencia, in which latter case the colour in general harmonises with the forehead band of the horse's trappings . . . The stripes of a Coachman's Vest run vertically. A sleeved vest is required for close fitting.   *Ibid.*

The collar could be step, roll or no collar.

Both Dress and Stable Vests are made with Sleeves.   *Ibid.*

A livery suit of the late nineteenth century of Mr. Gladstone's coachman has been preserved in the Cardiff Museum.

The coachman's driving outfit in the early nineteenth century would appear very old-fashioned, for he persisted in eighteenth century styles, even to the wearing of a wig. (See Frontispiece.)

A coachman in a tight silver wig.
W. M. Thackeray, *The History of Pendennis*, 1848

Every genuine coachman has his characteristic costume. His flaxen curls or wig, his low cocked hat, his plush breeches and his benjamin surtout, his clothes being well brushed and the . . . buttons in a state of high polish.
S. & S. Adams, *The Complete Servant*, 1825

The benjamin surtout was a loose overcoat, not so warm as the box coat but it was often caped. Vincent, in his *British Liveries*, 1894, tells us that

the old style of box coat [was] long enough to reach to the ankle, and made to button all down the front, so that the surplus width could be utilised to keep the legs of the coachman warm in severe weather. On the top of this was worn a series of deep capes . . . they being often arranged so that every other one was of a different colour, such as brown and blue, etc., etc. . . . . Although it formed a very good protection, Macintoshes and Driving Aprons have now taken its place. These are doubtless better for wet weather, but we think the coachman exposed to the cold weather would prefer the old style.

The macintosh was, however, an "exceptional part of a coachman's outfit" according to Vincent. The top hat began to appear about the middle of the nineteenth century.

The coachman's stable suit was usually a morning coat, close fitting trousers and a bowler hat.

THE POSTILLION's livery was usually very smart, as he was a rich man's servant when family coaches first appeared in the seventeenth century.

51. Coachman, double-breasted Box Coat, top hat with cockade, top boots, 1894.

52. Coachman's stable suit – morning coat, breeches and gaiters, bowler hat, 1894.

The Household Books of Sir Miles Stapleton in 1673 have the following entry.

> Disbursed for Jack Taylor (postillion) riding blue livery coat, etc.
> It. paid . . . for one yard and three quarters of blue broad cloth 00.12.00
> It. paid . . . for 3 yards of yellow paddua searge to line it with 00.10.00.
> It. paid . . . for buttons, lace, silke, stayes and making the livery coat in all 01.01.00
> Paid . . . for shammy leather doublet and blue cloth searge britches, with buttons, lineings, silk, thread, galloons ferrit ribbon and other things for making them up 01.00.08.

J. Charles Cox in *The Ancestor*, Vol. 3 (1902)

In 1757 the Duke of Bedford paid £5 each for livery suits which were made of orange cloth of the Russells' livery and "richly laced with gold and velvet" and decorated with nearly 100 gilt buttons. (G. Scott Thomson, *The Russells in Bloomsbury, 1669–1771*.)

Postillions wore short jackets and breeches. (Pls. 24 and 26.) In 1776, Louisa, Lady Stormont, describing her journey in a coach, wrote:

> They [the postillions] had scarlet jackets lined with silver . . . but what astonished me was their immense Jack Boots which hang on each side of the horse like two baskets, but I am convinced they are of great use as they are so thick that they will prevent them from hurting their legs in any accident.
> E. Maxtone Graham, *The Beautiful Mrs. Graham
> and the Cathcart Circle*, 1927

A foreigner travelling through England in 1782 was impressed by the English postchaises. He wrote:

> The postillions are particularly smart . . . The one we had wore his hair cut short, a round hat, and a brown jacket, of tolerable fine cloth with a nosegay in his bosom.
> *Travels of Carl Philipp Moritz in England, 1782*
> English translation 1795 by P. E. Matheson

The round hat became fashionable in the 1770's especially for riding. It had a round flat-topped crown varying in height and a flat uncocked brim. It was usually made of beaver. A round cap, however, was more usual.

The nineteenth century postillion's uniform was still an important feature of the family coach. See Pl. 24 (1848). Lord Frederick Hamilton wrote this of his boyhood in the 1860's:

> The crimson baroche with the six blacks and our own black and crimson liveries made a very smart turn-out indeed. . . . It was my consuming ambition to ride leader postillion and above all to wear the big silver coat-of-arms our postillions had strapped to the left sleeves of their short jackets, on a broad crimson band.
> *The Days Before Yesterday*, 1920

A postillion's dress wear was a short embroidered jacket with epaulettes and closed in front by a sham waistcoat stitched inside. On his head he wore a very elegant jockey cap over a wig with a queue. (See Footmen p. 89.)

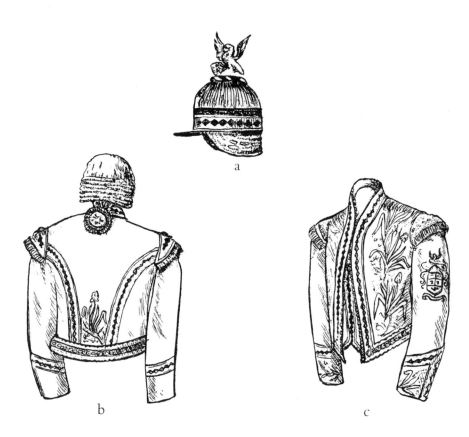

53. (a) Postillion's full dress cap, with wig showing below. (b) Back view of postillion's full dress jacket. The rosette on the collar represents the tie of the now extinct queue, once part of the wig. (c) Front view of postillion's full dress jacket with sham vest. His master's arms emblazoned on sleeve [1890–5].

THE TIGER

The "tiger" was a popular nineteenth century servant, and an important attendant on his employer when out driving alone. His duty was to hold the horse or horses when his employer left the driving seat to shop or walk around. (Pls. 25, 27.)

His livery was very smart with conspicuous trimmings whether he wore a riding coat (though he never rode), a jockey's coat, or a frock coat. Surtees describes a "neat" tiger in 1831, as wearing "a blue frock coat and leathers". *Jorrocks's Jaunts and Jollities.*

J. Couts in his *Practical Guide for the Cutting Room* in 1848 gives this description of a tiger's costume:

> A grey top hat with a gold band, a blue frock coat, a red waistcoat, breeches white or grey with a pin stripe and black or beige boots.

The tiger was always very small whatever his age. He is faithfully remembered in Barham's *Ingoldsby Legends* in 1840.

> His Tiger Tim was clean of limb
> His boots were polished, his jacket was trim,
> With a very smart tie in his smart cravat,
> And a little cockade on the top of his hat,
> Tallest of boys or shortest of men
> He stood in his stockings just four feet ten.

Because he was small he sometimes had to act as a page also. The following is a letter purporting to have been written by a youthful lady's maid in an upstart Bloomsbury family, concerning a tiger. The letter appeared in *Punch* in 1841:

> Theodore – in the morning he's a tigger drest in a tite froc-cote, top-boots buxkin small closes [breeches] and stuck up behind Master Augustusses cab. In the evening he gives up the tigger and comes out as a paige, in a fansy jacket with too rose of guilt buttings . . . and being such a small chap, you may suppose they [the ladies] can never make enuff of him.

A lad doubling the parts of tiger and page is shown in Pl. 27.

THE GROOM IN CHARGE OF HORSES

In humbler families or when actually at work, the groom, in the middle ages and even in the sixteenth century, wore a loose tunic-like garment with a belt, long hose and a hat or cap – the garb of a typical working man.

In upper class families at least by the sixteenth century, grooms of the stable were wearing livery. As we have seen (Fig. 4) in Turberville's *Booke of Hunting*, 1575, the Queen's grooms are depicted in the fashion, wearing trunk hose with the royal badge embroidered on the front of their doublets. Milton, in *Paradise Lost* (1667), wrote:

> The tedious pomp that waits
> On princes, when their rich retinue long

Of horses led, and *grooms* besmeared with gold
Dazzles the crowd.

which suggests a grand livery.

In the eighteenth century jackets, which were normal wear for the working classes, and breeches were worn. The *Morning Post* of September 18th, 1788, suggests that "a brown jacket with a multiple of pockets on each side, that reaches from the bottom to the top" was the kind worn by "a set of grooms".

In the nineteenth century the uniform for "undress" was in some cases:

<blockquote>

Jacket with two pockets
Waistcoat with vertical stripes
Breeches, buff or grey
Gaiters matching the coat
Stock red with white stripes
Top hat.

Dress   Coat red and waistcoat
Breeches green
Top boots
Top hat black with gold band.

</blockquote>

Costumes for grooms in 1848 are shown in Plates 28 and 29 and another for 1894 in Fig. 56(a).

Surtees, in *Handley Cross*, 1854, describes:

> . . . . a groom's drab frock coat reaching down to his heels, a sky-blue waistcoat, patent cord breeches with grey worsted stockings and slippers, airing a pair of very small mud-stained top-boots before the fire.

The length of this groom's frock coat was a bit exaggerated.

Stable leggings had to be made in a special way. They

54. Groom, in short tunic, hat worn over coif, light ankle boots, thirteenth century.

55. Groom in belted, working man's coat tied in front. Old-fashioned long hose (tights) with codpiece, 1563.

56. (*Left*) "Groom, S.B. frock coat, as worn for riding behind a lady, the belt signifying mounted duty and not worn on the box. Belt brown leather. The groom's frock should be three inches shorter than the coachman's and should not have cross pockets, but pleat pockets. Shoulder cords are put on for mourning." (*Right*) Coachman in S.B. frock, top boots, top hat with cockade, 1894.

54

55

56

have no tongue . . . are wider at the ankle than a close measurement and they are sprung out at the sides to allow them to be over the tie of the shoes . . . Mud boots are longer leggings which go over the boots or shoes and are cut by the same method.

W. D. F. Vincent, op. cit.

STABLE BOYS

The Household Accounts of Sir John Howard show that in 1464 his stable boys received from time to time shirts, doublets, hose [i.e. leg wear in the form of tights], shoes, and boots which were "fore-footed". A few received gowns which were over-garments worn for warmth. The stable boy called Jenyn was supplied, in 1465, with

> a doublet, a payr of hosen and iii shepes scynnys to make him a jacket . . . I payr of botys.

57. Stable boy (holding the horse) in long plain tunic. Thirteenth century.

Stable boys in the eighteenth and nineteenth centuries usually wore a brown jacket or a waistlength coatee like a jockey's. When working in the stables a man might put on a washable overall shaped like a country man's smock. A stable boy "dressed up to the nines" is described by Surtees in *Handley Cross*:

> Stephen's lad, dressed in an old blue dress-coat of his master's with a blue and white striped livery waistcoat, top boots and drab cords [breeches] and having a cockade in his hat, kept walking the horse up and down.   1854

The grandeur of the clothes supplied to the royal household servants in Queen Elizabeth's funeral procession (1603) is shown in Pl. 30. All are in mourning. Note the black cloaks, black hats and white neck wear and gloves. Ruffs are worn by some of the higher grade servants who also carry swords, e.g. Messengers of the Chamber. The sword hilts are gold, but the scabbards are black. The lower grade servants such as the Children of the Almonry wear white collars (bands) and no beards.

CHAPTER FIVE

Women servants' costume – special features

UPPER RANKS OF WOMEN SERVANTS

THE WAITING GENTLEWOMAN OR LADY'S MAID

This attendant was among the highest ranking servants and dressed accordingly. M. St. Clare Byrne in her delightful book *The Elizabethan Home*, has given us quotations from "Two Dialogues by Claudius Hollyband and Peter Erondell". Here we find a rare description of what a waiting gentlewoman wore in 1605. She has to dress in a hurry and exclaims:

> Good Lord! What shall I do?... I pray thee... help me [to the chamber maid]... to put on my gowne, give me that Rebato as it is, I will pin it anone, I have not leisure to do it now: I cannot find my kertle nor my aprone.

58. Lady's maid doing her mistress's hair. Ground length kirtle, similar to that of her mistress and veil head-dress, *c.* 1340.

59. "Protector and Protected". Lady's maid, walking behind her mistress. Both wear crinolines and "Empire bonnets", i.e. small with no "curtain" at the back, but in contrast to the lady's fur jacket and frilled skirt, the maid wears a cloak and her skirt is plain, 1866.

The rebato was a white collar wired up to stand fan-wise, round the back of the neck of a low-necked bodice to which it was pinned. This would never have been worn by a lower ranking servant maid.

Gowns were usually open in front from the waist down, revealing the kirtle. This style, together with the rebato, was slightly old fashioned, being the style of the end of the sixteenth century. At all periods the lady's maid's costume, like the valet's, was very smart, but discreetly a little less dressy than their employer's, especially when the two are seen together. This is very obvious in our Fig. 59 "Protector and Protected" (1866). They both wear "Empire bonnets", but the maid's is untrimmed. In contrast to the lady's fur jacket and frilled skirt,

60. Lady's maid in plaid dress, short apron and small cap with ribbons, helping her mistress into a cage crinoline, 1858.

61. Nurse in elegant mob cap, but dress in marked contrast to the up-to-date *Directoire* lines of her mistress's, 1796.

the maid has a cloak, shaped like a shawl and her skirt is quite plain. (Fig. 59 (1866).) Frances Trollope, on the other hand, emphasises the elegance of the lady's maid in comparison with other servants. Elegance is again the keynote in our frontispiece. The following illustrations show the various lady's maids' attire from the Middle Ages to the nineteenth century. See Fig. 60, Pl. 31 (1810), Pl. 32 (1480) and Pl. 38 (1840) and Frontispiece (1827).

NURSERY AND SCHOOLROOM STAFF

The status of a *head nurse* has generally been that of an upper ranking servant. As such she sometimes dressed like a contemporary gentle-woman, though much more simply than her mistress and less fashion-ably than the lady's maid.

Unless very superior, a nurse might even, like the parlourmaid, wear a print dress in the morning (Pl. 35(a)) and she nearly always wore an apron.

Throughout the eighteenth and nineteenth centuries the children's nurse wore a cap and apron. See Pls. 35, 36, 37. The cap was generally a mob cap (Figs. 62, 63), or in some cases a daintier small cap and occasionally one with streamers (Figs. 64 and 69).

Out of doors a bonnet and shawl were usual (Figs. 65, 66).

Here is what some children thought of their nurse in 1893.

> We consider nurse a very cross person . . . Her aprons are as stiff as the nursery tea-tray, besides being the same plain shape, and she will wear the tightest and sternest caps that ever were seen . . . Bobby . . . did wish that something would soon happen to nurse's best cap. He said it looked so hard; her caps were all strictish, but her Sunday cap was savage.
>
> Frances E. Crompton *The Gentle Heritage*

The *Mother's Magazine* (1889–90) tells us that

> Little babies are always dressed entirely in white and the nurse who brings the baby into the drawing room is nearly always dressed in some similar material. The effect is decidedly pleasing and the baby's finery is preserved from contact with any material which can injure it.

White, however, was not very common for a nurse's dress; any sober colour was worn, the baby's "finery" being "preserved" by the bib of the apron. This too might be frilled with matching "finery". See Pl. 36.)

62

63

64

1. *Above* Livery hats – top hats with cockades. 1892.
Advertisement in *The Queen* 19th March 1892. Reproduced in *Victorian Advertisements*, 1968, L. de Vries and James Laver
(*Below*) Negro page's silver collar, 1680.
Godfrey Kneller. Portrait of Capt. Thomas Lucy [with his page] (detail).
Charlcote Park. Courtesy of the National Trust.

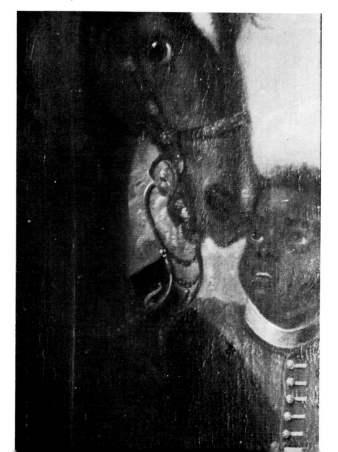

2. "A Neat Turnout". Black footman in evening dress suit, tailcoat with epaulettes, knee breeches, white stockings, slippers and top hat with cockade, 1830s.
Contemporary print, pubd. by Wm. Spooner, London.

3. Negro page-boy. Fancy turban with feather, silver collar (would be engraved with employer's name); livery shoulder knot, 1732–4.
Engraving by W. Hogarth, Harlot.s Progress II (detail).

4. Black footman, bare-headed (right). Black page with turban and feather (extreme left), 1748. Engraving after W. Hogarth, Marriage a-la-Mode IV (detail).

5. (*Below*) Heads of six of Hogarth's own servants. They have a humble appearance, the older, if not both men, having natural hair instead of wigs; even the younger has neckwear in seventeenth century style. The maids have bonnet-shaped mob caps, 1750–5.
Painting by Hogarth reproduced by kind permission of the Trustees of the Tate Gallery.

a   b   c   d   e   f

6. "High Life below stairs". 1772. From left to right:

(a) *Footman* in fashionable "frock" and a "solitaire" of black ribbon round his neck (very stylish).

(b) *Housemaid* in a day cap known as a "dormeuse", very popular in the 1770s, but she wears the customary neckerchief and an apron.

(c) *Cook* in mob cap, neckerchief; she shows her apron strings.

(d) *Lady's maid* in protective shoulder negligé, dainty shoes and apron. Her bergère hat on the floor.

(e) *Valet* wears a wig.

(f) *Laundry woman* wears a jacket bodice, otherwise dressed like the cook.

George Paston, *Social Caricatures in the Eighteenth Century* [1905], PI.CXCI Collett Pinxt, Caldwell, Sculpt.

7. Figure of a housemaid in very smart fashionable attire. Bodice with slashed sleeves and wings, double-laced cuffs and lace-edged cap. Embroidered skirt and apron caught up to reveal this. She wears a falling ruff, 1643.

A figure in cut-out board – in Stoneleigh Abbey. Photo. *Connoisseur*, March 1942.

8. Valet wearing elegant suit and draped cloak but ruff instead of the newer style of neckwear worn by his masters. He stands bare headed, holding his hat in their presence, but wears a sword (note its hilt). 1598.
Isaac Oliver, "The Brothers Browne" (detail). Portrait at Burghley House, Stamford, Marquis of Exeter.

9. The parlourmaid has distended her skirt with wire to imitate a crinoline, 1863–4.

10. "A Dashing Turn-Out". Page in coatee with vestigal tails, plentiful buttons, white stripe to trousers, top hat with side strings and cockade, 1843.
Hand tinted lithograph, author's collection.

11. Chamberlain (i.e. valet) in pale lilac long tunic caught in by girdle at waist, bare headed. He helps his master to put on his hose [stockings] 1320. *Queen Mary's Psalter*, B.M. MS. Roy 2 B VII f.72v.

12. Valet starching his master's neck wear. The valet is in breeches, c.1830. "The Acme of Fashion". Hand coloured print pub. by McCleary, author's collection.

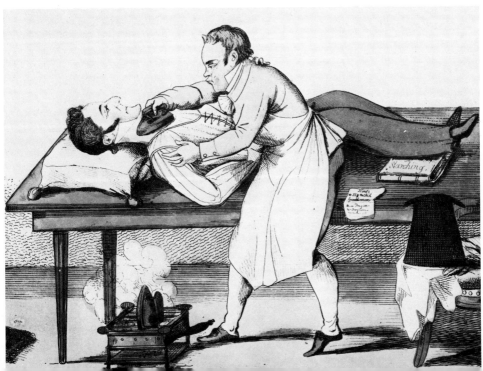

a   b   c   d

13. Servants interviewed at Register Office, 1769. (a) and (c) Maids of all work, wearing long aprons and typical neckerchiefs; (b) Coachman, blue livery coat, elderly style wig; (d) Footman with natural hair. Engraving by M. Darby, coloured impression, author's collection.

14. (*Left*) Smart footman in green coat, yellow breeches, pink waistcoat and wearing a bag wig. (*Right*) Country footman in out-door attire, blue coat trimmed with buff and gold, shoulder knot, red breeches, buff and gold waistcoat, black "bicorne" gold edged hat, cockade. He carries a staff. 1812. "Yorkshire Bumkin's Mistake" by G. Woodward, Guildhall Library.

15. Footman's indoor livery: (*Left*) *Undress* vlue coatee with grey epaulettes, waistcoat with red and white horizontal stripes. Black pantaloons. Hair natural. He holds a napkin. (*Right*) *Dress* "A knight of the Shoulder Knot". White dress coat, collar and cuffs red, gold buttons and trimming, red waistcoat edged with gold, black breeches, buckled over the knee with gold band. White stockings and pumps. Hair powdered white. 1848.
J. Couts, *Practical Guide for the Tailor's Cutting Room*, pl. XXI, 1848.

16. Footman's outdoor livery: (*Left*) *Full dress*, blue tail coat, yellow collar and cuffs, shoulder knot. Yellow waistcoat and breeches. White stockings, buckled shoes. "Bicorne" hat with cockade, white gloves. He holds a staff. (*Right*) *Undress*, maroon caped great coat piped with red: brass buttons. Black top hat with gold band: grey leggings.
J. Couts, *Practical Guide for the Tailor's Cutting Room*, p. XXII, 1848.

17. Three servers in coloured tunics, holding green napkins. 1325–50.
"Marriage of the Lamb", Trinity College, Cambridge, MS. R. 162 f. 22.

18. Cook in white apron, red jacket, white hose ("tights"), old fashioned
ankle strap shoes, fifteenth century.
Facsimile of the *Ellesmere Chaucer*, Vol. 1, Manchester, 1911.

19. (*Left*) Cook wearing primitive apron (i.e. cloth tucked into belt) adjusts a log on the fire. (*Right*) Cook turns the spit, *c.* 1340.

20. Cook beside cauldron has a grey apron, short pale tunic with cuffs turned up, green hose, a beard. Man chopping vegetables wears a short yellow tunic, but no apron. Man stirring cauldron has a natural-coloured tunic, grey buff apron, *c.* 1340.
Luttrell Psalter, B.M. MS. Add. 42130, f. 206b, v. 207: detail.

21. Kitchen Scene. At the table the head cook "instructing a Young Man in the Art of Carving". The young man wears protective sleeves. On the left "A Lady presenting her Servant with the *Universal Family Cook*", a book of instructions. Two kitchen boys at the oven wear very long aprons; one has pantaloons, and a queue wig, the other has breeches and natural hair. A kitchen maid operates the turnspit and also bastes. She wears a long dress, a mob cap and an apron. 1795.

Wm. A. Henderson, *Housekeepers Instructor or Universal Family Cook*, 1795. (Frontispiece, drawn and engraved by Collinger.)

22. (*Above*) The Clerk of the Kitchen bringing
in dishes has a belted tunic and purse for accounts
attached. The cup bearer has a loose surcote over
tight-sleeved "cote". He carries his embroidered
napkin round his neck, *c.* 1340. (*Below*) Carver:
apron tucked into tunic belt, chaperon-type
head-dress, *c.* 1340.
Luttrell Psalter, B.M. MS. Add. 42130 ff. 208,
207v.

24. "Old Whip and Young Spurs". (*Left*) Postillion in blue jacket, silver buttons, gold collar, cuffs and belt. White breeches, top boots with gold tops. White breeches, top boots with gold tops. White jockey cap with black band. (*Right*) Coachman, fawn box coat, having capes edged with red. Black top hat with fawn band. He wears a white wig with two rows of curls. 1848.

J. Couts, *Practical Guide for the Tailor's Cutting Room*, 1848.

23. (*Facing page*) "The Scullion of Christ Church". He wears a brown coat, (patched and split) brown cap tied with red strings. On his hands are blue mittens of a curious design, possibly worn as protection when polishing pewter, *c.* 1688.

Portrait by J. Riley. Reproduced by courtesy of the Governing Body of Christ Church, Oxford.

25. (*Left*) Page and (*right*) Tiger. Page in typical livery. Tiger in elegantly waisted blue coat, red waistcoat, white corduroy breeches, top hat with gold band and cockade, top boots. 1848.

J. Couts, *Practical Guide for the Tailor's Cutting Room*, 1848.

26. "The New Gig." Postillion in short jacket with shoulder epaulettes, vertically striped waistcoat, jack boots. 1781.

"The New Gig" by Colley, 1781, reproduced in George Paston, *Social Caricatures of the Eighteenth Century*, 1905.

27. Tiger to lady in crinoline. He wears a top hat with side strings from brim to crown and buttons as worn by a page, so possibly this is a page acting as a tiger. 1858. "Crinoline, 1858 Brompton." Contemporary print, author's collection.

28. (*Left*) Groom in "undress" clothes, jacket, breeches, gaiters and plain top hat. (*Right*) Groom in dress clothes, frock coat with shoulder epaulettes, breeches and top boots. Top hat with cockade. 1848.
J. Couts, *Practical Guide for the Tailor's Cutting Room*, 1848.

29. (*Left*) Groom in short grey frock coat, vertically striped waistcoat, white breeches, grey gaiters, top hat. (*Right*) Coachman in grey overcoat without capes but prominent shoulder knot with long cords, yellow collar, cuffs and pockets with white buttons, top hat. 1848.
J. Couts, *Practical Guide for the Tailor's Cutting Room* [1848].

30. Servants of Queen Elizabeth I at her funeral, all wearing black. Two bare-headed "Querries" lead her horse. "Messengers" in mourning cloaks wear swords. "Children" of the almonry, woodyard, scullery, etc., being lads, lack swords.

B.M. MS. Add. 35324 f. 28 (early Eighteenth Century).

31. Lady's maid in high-waisted blue dress with a chemisette fill-in to the low neck line. Long white apron, mob cap with red ribbon, red slippers. Her mistress in white negligé, is waiting to be fitted with a wig. 1810.

"Progress of the Toilet, the Wig", drawn and engraved by J. Gillray.

32. Lady in fashionable trained gown (held up showing her kirtle) and a steeple head-dress with very long veil. Her lady's maid in similar gown, but no train and a similar but shorter head-dress, follows carrying parcels. One porter, carrying a trunk, has the "points" (ties) of his hose untrussed (untied) at the back showing his naked buttocks. Late Fifteenth Century.
Froissart's Chronicle, B.M. MS. Harl. 4380 f. 189v.

33. (a) and (b) Blanche Parry, who was nurse to Queen Elizabeth as a baby and afterwards her hand maid. She is fashionably dressed, in her ruffs, necklace, etc., but modestly she wears no farthingale. In (b) she is seen handing a jewel to the Queen. Both effigies *c.* 1590.

(a) Effigy on tomb of Blanche Parry, St. Margaret's Church, Westminster. Photo: National Monuments Record. (b) Effigy of Blanche Parry, Bacton Church, Herefordshire. Photo by courtesy of F. C. Morgan.

a

b

34. French governess (3rd from left) in fashionable attire. Note the crucifix,
decorative apron and arch expression. Holding the boy's hand is the housemaid wearing a babet cap. 1840.
Frances Trollope, *The Life and Adventures of Michael Armstrong*, edn 1840
(detail of illustration by A. Kervieu).

35. (*Left*) Nurse in the morning; long print dress and apron with bib pinned to bodice: no shoulder straps. Small cap. (*Right*) Same nurse in the evening; black dress, bibbed apron with shoulder straps. 1900.
Frances Crompton, *Master Harry's Book*, illustrated edn 1900.

36. Nurse in cap and apron, bibbed and frilled over the shoulders. 1900.
Photo: private collection.

37. (*Facing page*) "Ready for the Party."
Nurse in black dress, short checked apron, cap trimmed with lace. 1866.
Portrait of his little daughter by James Hayllar.

38. Seated in the centre is the magnificent housekeeper wearing a very fashionably shaped print dress, a babet cap trimmed with ribbon, a spreading collar and a short apron. Behind her the "lordly butler", and the liveried footman with shoulder knot. Fat cook behind footman. Extreme right kitchen maid, in babet cap and apron. Extreme left the lady's maid in decorative apron and dressed "with all the elegant superiority of attire which marks the station". 1840.

Frances Trollope, *The Life and Adventures of Michael Armstrong*, edn 1840. (A Kervieu's illustration of Michael's introduction to the household staff.)

39. "The Old Housekeeper." In a dark dress, light shawl and a white old-fashioned cap frilled and tied under the chin. She wears spectacles. No chatelaine as she is not on duty. 1870.
Portrait by Henry Stacey Marks, 1870. Photo: by kind permission of Messrs Newman Galleries, London.

40. Maid cup-bearer, wearing a long pale lilac gown. She kneels and is bare headed, because of her present occupation. Hair arranged with "bosses" round the ears. The musician playing a viol wears a short orange coloured tunic. 1320.
Queen Mary's Psalter, B.M. MS. Roy. 2B VII f. 168v.

41. "An English Family at Tea." Parlourmaid in fashionable wide skirt and "pinner" cap with the lappets pinned up. Large white apron, *c.* 1720.
By unknown British artist. Reproduced by kind permission of the Trustees of the Tate Gallery.

42. Parloumaid, afternoon black dress with fashionable sleeves, starched
bibbed apron, cap with long white streamers. 1894.
"Five O'clock Tea" by William Powell Frith, 1894. Photo. by courtesy of
Messrs Newman Galleries, London.

43. (*Below*) Typical parlourmaids in dark dresses, elegant small white caps and clean starched aprons, also white cuffs and collars, *c.* 1900.
Photo. from the Mansell Collection, London.

44. (*Facing page*) Domestic servant Holmes aet 96. Plain gown, large "neckerchief" and coif in the fashion of her youth and very plain. Page boy smartly dressed in the fashion of the day. 1686.
John Riley, Portrait of Bridget Holmes aet. 96. Reproduced by gracious permission of H.M. the Queen.

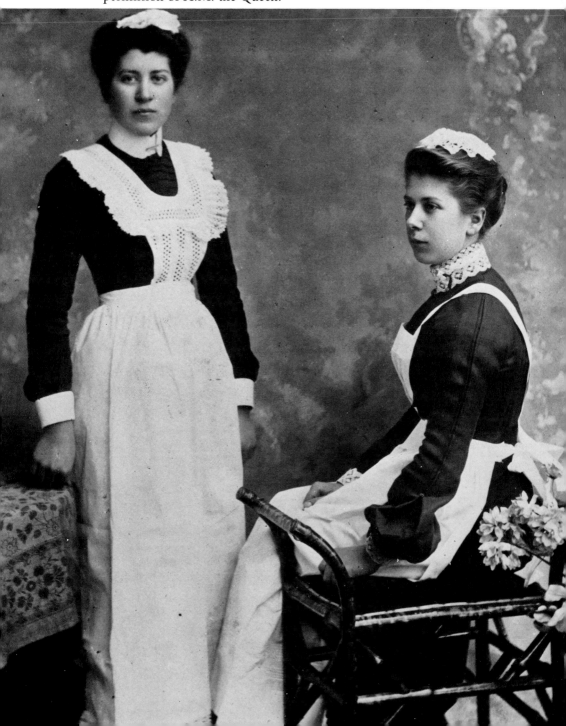

45. Cook wearing functional apron and the long kirtle and veil of her period. Early Fourteenth Century.
B.M. MS. Roy. 10 E IV, f. 109v.

46. Cook-maid in black dress, bibbed apron and elegant day cap trimmed and tied with ribbon, c. 1830.
Reproduced in G. M. Young, *Early Victorian England*, Vol. 1, Pub. 1934.

47. (a) Cook-maid wearing a smart black hat over a white coif, an apron over a fashionable polonaise dress, i.e. with an ovrrskirt bunched up behind. Ankle length underskirt. 1772.
(b) Cook-maid in mob cap with green ribbon, yellow neckerchief with red spots, white dress with pink stripes, white apron, red shoes. 1800.
(a) Engraving by Caldwell after painting by Brandoin, B.M. George Catalogue No. 4603.
(b) Drawn and engraved by G. Woodward (detail). Coloured impression. B.M. George Catalogue No. 9646.

48. Primitive aprons "Who was then the gentleman?"
Adam and Eve design on Bristol Delft blue-dash charger, *c.* 1680, ex author's
collection.

65

66

62. Nanny in old-fashioned jacket bodice, neckerchief, mob cap and apron, 1816.

63. Nurse wearing a "babet" style of mob-cap (cf. Fig. 87), bibbed apron and skirt bunched up and tucked through placket hole showing long petticoat. Large neckerchief, 1823.

64. Nurse, black dress, white apron and small cap, 1856.

65. The small boy "ran and hid his face in his Nurse's Cloak". The cloak is a bye-gone fashion and the nurse's bonnet is simpler than the lady's. *c.* 1825.

66. Nursery maid in outdoor bonnet and shawl. "Nursery maids are seldom without a smile upon their faces out of doors . . . The devotees at the shrine of the nursery maid, in her daily walks are numerous, from the pert butterman's boy and rosy butcher's lad, to the powdered old gentleman with his walking stick and spectacles", 1845.

67. Smart nurse wearing white dress with fashionable sleeves and very small bonnet, also correct style, 1899.

119

68. Nursemaid in small cap, head nurse in elaborate day cap, print dress and
apron, 1855.

69. Head nurse in cap with streamers, apron and slightly trained skirt, 1874.
A royal christening. Queen Victoria and the Prince of Wales are on the right.

When her charges grew up, a head nurse might be promoted to the lady's maid's post and her attire then took on a much more stylish air. We find an example in Blanche Parry, who was "nanny" to Queen Elizabeth I. Her effigy in St. Margaret's Church, Westminster (Pl. 33(a) (1589)), shows her in the height of fashion. According to her epitaph she served the Queen faithfully "from her Highness birth" and continued to do so all her life. She died at the age of 82, in 1589–90. When no longer required as a "nanny" she became "Gentlewoman of Queen Elizabeth's most honourable bedchamber and Keeper of her Maties juells". Blanche Parry's heart was buried in Bacton Church, Herefordshire. Her monument is shown in Pl. 33(b). The rhymed epitaph reads as follows:

I lyvde allweys as handmaede to a Quene
In Chamber Chief my tyme dyd overpasse
. . . .
Not doubtynge wante whyllste that my Mystres lyvde
In woman's state whose cradell saw I rockte

70. Governess in lady-like dress of her period and poke bonnet. The little pupils in similar outfits, 1820.

Her servannte then as when her croune atcheeved
And so remaende tyll death my doore had knockte. *c.* 1589

The rocking of the cradle refers to her early years as Queen Elizabeth's "nanny".

A cut above the average nurse was the older children's governess in the nineteenth century. This gentlewoman would avoid any functional kind of dress, but she could not, as a rule, afford good clothes and did not receive the cast-offs of her mistress. Thus her chief distinguishing mark was an air that combined the ladylike with the drab and unassuming. Somewhat more dashing, she might be, if she was French. (Pl. 34.)

THE HOUSEKEEPER

Except in the great households of earlier times, the controller, both of the servants and the supplies, was usually an elderly matron, the housekeeper.

71. Nursery governess in plain dress, teaching the child on her right. "Mrs Melville [and her two little girls] listened with interest", 1845.

72. Superior governess in the sheath-like dress of her date, 1878.

Typically she wore an apron, but her bonnet or cap, as seen at the end of the nineteenth century, was deliberately out of date, as a sign of dignity and discretion, like a widow's, far removed from the fly away cap of the maid's uniform, or the smartness of a lady's maid (Pls. 38, 39). A high-necked stiff dress with a large brooch was characteristic.

The almost universal feature of her dress was the chatelaine dangling from her waistband. On this she kept the keys of all the store cupboards. By this symbol of office we can always recognise her, even when, as on the frontispiece, she wears an unusually frivolous air.

THE PARLOURMAID

This term was applied to a somewhat superior maid servant, in the nineteenth century. She was frequently in contact with her mistress, and in the absence of a footman she might wait at table, usher in guests or even answer the door. Consequently she had to appear tidy and well dressed at all times. Her counterpart in earlier days was called a serving maid or, in a rare instance, she appeared as a cup bearer. See Pl. 40 (1320). Her white apron does not seem to have been typical until the seventeenth or eighteenth centuries. See Pl. 41 (*c.* 1720).

In the nineteenth century, changing in the afternoon became an established rule and at tea time parlourmaids had to re-appear in black. Fig. 76(a) and (b). Towards the end of the century the apron had a bib secured by cross straps behind: a frill was sometimes allowed. Although ladies in the 1860's were beginning to discard indoor head wear, this was the one fashion denied to maid servants. Indoor caps had to be

73. Housekeeper in cap and apron, wearing a chatelaine, 1893.

75. Serving maid wearing a surcoat over a long blue kirtle, and a pale pink apron. Hair in plaits turned up round the ears, with a very narrow fillet worn across the forehead, a contrast to the elaborate headdresses of the period. Fifteenth Century after 1426.

74. Elegant parlourmaid answering the door. She wears a cap with streamers, a frilled apron, black dress, 1894.

76. (a) Parlourmaid in fashionable black dress with kick-up sleeves, cap with streamers and apron with fancy bib. The mistress by now does not wear an indoor cap, 1893–4. (b) Parlourmaid, black dress, apron, small cap, fashionable hair style, 1893–4.

worn by all. The following is what a lady considered the correct outfit for a good maid in 1847.

> A nice plain cotton gown of only one colour – being a nice spot on a dark green ground – . . . a good strong serviceable half-a-crown Dunstable straw bonnet trimmed very plainly . . . a . . . quilled net cap under it; . . . a tidy plain muslin collar over a . . . black and white plaid shawl . . . I felt quite charmed at seeing her dressed so thoroughly like what a respectable servant ought to be.
>
> H. & A. Mayhew The Greatest Plague of Life

Unfortunately the maid soon fell short of what was expected of her! When dressed for duty she wore:

> A fly-away, starched-out imitation Balzierne gown of a bright ultramarine, picked out with white flowers – on each side of her head a bunch of long ringlets like untwisted bell-ropes, and a blonde lace cap with cherry coloured streamers about a yard long.

This in spite of the order that "no ringlets, followers or sandals" would be allowed. (Fig. 77.) "Followers" were, of course, a problem with all

77

George Cruikshank

78. Cook in cap and apron, reproved by her mistress for allowing a "follower" into the kitchen. "It's only my cousin", 1847.

77.(*Facing*) Parlourmaid in black dress, apron and small cap worn far back to make room for the curls. Lady of the house exclaims: "Hoity toity, indeed! Go and put up those curls, directly if you please. How dare you imitate me in that manner? Impertinence!" 1852.

79. Housekeeper at desk, wearing the typical housekeeper's day cap, and chatelaine suspended from her belt. She also wears spectacles (see pl. 39). Two housemaids facing her and a fat cook at the back. All wear caps and aprons. The cook's has a bib and her sleeves are rolled up, 1851.

maids. (Figs. 78 and 79.) The cap, so essential, might be a mob cap in the old-fashioned style, tied under the chin, or a cap with streamers hanging behind (Pl. 42), or finally a tiny object perched on the top of the head (Pl. 43). Coloured ribbons were allowed at times, the only pieces of finery to which a young servant might aspire, perhaps because the men liked them. It was certainly one man's choice in 1842.

I like to be waited on by a neat-handed Phillis of a girl in her nice fitting gown and a pink ribbon in her cap.
W. M. Thackeray *The Tribulations of a Gentleman in search of a Manservant* 1842

The outdoor dress was usually a shawl and a straw bonnet over the indoor cap.

Even lower ranking women servants, unlike the men, had no regulation costumes which might indicate their particular kind of work, until the reign of Queen Victoria, when some conventions became established.

Generally speaking, the ordinary maid servant's dress conformed to that of the better off working class in that it was the style of the day, with certain limitations. The materials were cheaper and the designs simpler than those of the gentry.

Throughout the Middle Ages a lady wore a full length dress known as a kirtle, often tight fitting, and in addition an overgarment, such as a supertunic or "surcote", later called a gown, so that the kirtle was almost hidden from view. The maid, on the other hand, wore a loose fitting kirtle, generally without a surcote which would have been cumbersome for her work. For extra warmth a cloak was preferred. From the ninth to the twelfth centuries these were usually closed all round and thigh-length, but subsequently worn open and longer. Skirts were often only ankle-length and frequently tucked up out of the way, but long skirts and even trains were permissible. Head-dresses were much less elaborate than those worn by their mistresses, the simple medieval veil and the hood being usual; but some sort of head covering was essential except for the very young girl.

The medieval peasant working on the farm often wore a bibless apron. (Those in the fourteenth century were frequently embroidered.) Servants at that time seem to have used them little except when cooking.

Fig. 80 from a fifteenth century manuscript shows a chambermaid who is beating a mattress.

And sche that bare the staff anon
Ffro bed to bed sche is agon
. . . .
And with clothes cleene and white
Sche spradde hem over by delyte.
B.M. MS. Tib. A VII (A poem trans. by J. Lydgate 1426)

This woman has hitched up her rather short kirtle and wears blue working gloves, but she does not wear an apron.

The sixteenth century "maid of all work" continued with her kirtle and apron and was obliged to forego a farthingale when this became the fashion for her mistress from 1545 to the 1620's. This enormously distended hooped petticoat would have hampered the maid's work beyond endurance. Thomas Churchyard in 1575 describes in his *Churchyard's Chippes* a model servant as she cleans the house.

> And at her gyrdle in a band
> A jolly bunch of keyes she wore
> Her petticoat fine laced before
> Her taile tucke up in trymmest gies
> A napkin hanging o'er her eies
> To keep of[f] dust and drosse of walles
> That often from the windowes falles.

The "taile" was a short train to her skirt.

The maid also had holiday clothes, some of which she had made herself.

> Two fayre new kirtles to her backe
> The one was blue the other black . . . .
> She had three smockes, she had no less
> Four rayles and eke five kerchers fayre
> Of hose and shoes she had a payre . . . .
> She would go bare-foote for to save
> Her shoes and hose for they were deere.   Ibid.

The smocks were her chemises and the rayles were waist length light capes.

80. Chambermaid. Her pink kirtle or "cote", worn without surcote, girdled so as to be well above ankles (not like a lady's). Old fashioned white veil head-dress, a pleated barbe covering her neck and sides of face. Blue gauntlet gloves (see text). From MS. itself. Fifteenth century after 1426.

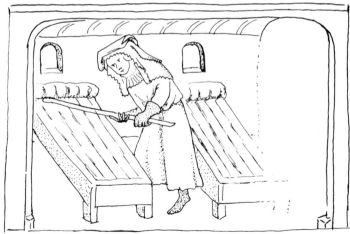

81. Housemaid sweeping away flies. She wears a
bibless apron, a neckerchief and sleeves rolled up, hair
tied back but no cap! *c.* 1556.

In wealthy households women servants were often well dressed. The
following list is a complete outfit supplied to "a mayde" in Queen
Elizabeth's Court.

A black fryse cassocke [a long loose overcoat] with poyntinge rebande and
two fustian pockettes and lyned collar and ventes: sixe lynen Aprons: one
Apron of fuste mockado: foure cutt koyves [coif decorated with cut-work]
foure cutt kercheves, foure other kercheves: two peire of hose: a wastecoate
of red kersey: a felte hatte: foure peires of showes: foure cawles[1] and foure
smockes: two petycoates, one red cloth th' other stammel frysado, upper-
bodied with mockado, lyned with fustian, frenged with cruell, lyned about
the skyrtes with bayes. (1575)   B.M. MS. Egerton 2806 f. 92

[1] The caul was a trellis-work coif or skull cap often made with silk thread and
sometimes lined with silk. It was worn by young women.

In 1607, Shakespeare refers to a "malkin", a kitchen maid, who like the scullion already mentioned was a dirty servant.

> Your prattling nurse
> Into a rapture lets her baby cry
> While she chats him; the kitchen malkin pins
> Her richest lockram 'bout her reechy[2] neck
> Clambering the walls to eye him.
> *Coriolanus* II i

Lockeram was a coarse linen worn by the poorer classes. In this case it was probably the malkin's neckerchief.

But on the whole, the servant girls were clean and dressed simply, being discouraged from finery, even by Sumptuary Laws (cf. p. 63). A good example of simple neatness is shown in the portrait in Pl. 44.

In the eighteenth century maids in the country appear to have dressed very simply. Their skirts were long, often bunched up behind to get them out of the way, but the hoop petticoat, so universal from *c.* 1710 to 1780, was avoided. Aprons were essential and head wear consisted of a mob cap, or plain round cap, and out of doors a limp hood, worn over the mob or sometimes a bergère hat. See Pl. 13(a) and (c) (1769). The hood might be separate or attached to a cloak. Plain black leather shoes were usual and out of doors, as a protection from dirt, these would be worn with pattens. The materials generally used for maids' aprons and caps were cottons, and printed linens for their dresses. Parson Woodforde in 1784 wrote "married my old Maid Eliz Claxton to Charles Cary . . . She was dressed in a Linnen Gown that my Niece gave her some time back". *The Diary of a Country Parson*, Vol. II, ed. John Beresford. In 1795 there was a letter in the *Times* complaining of the waste of flour used in the starching of servants' white dresses and kerchiefs. Sophie von la Roche in *Sophie in London* describes a maid's outfit thus: "Black taminy petticoat rather stiff and heavily starched". This was an underpetticoat giving fullness to the skirt of her dress which she wore "with" a "long English calico or linen frock . . . and white apron, black shoes". 1786. A maid's frock at this time implied a back-fastening dress of thin material.

Domestics in London and in towns, however, tended to be better dressed than their country cousins. A general impression is given by

[2] Dirty.

J. W. Archenholz, a foreigner, who wrote this in *A Picture of England*, in 1787 (translated in 1797):

> The appearance of the female domestics will perhaps astonish a foreign visitor more than anything in London. They are in general handsome and well clothed; their dress has the appearance of some taste . . . They are usually clad in gowns well adjusted to their shapes, and hats adorned with ribbands. There are some who even wear silk and satin when they are dressed.

In the nineteenth century the servant maid's dress varied according to her duties and her employer's status. Cotton was now becoming cheap and was also easy to wash, so that the "print dress" was her usual working attire. Her aprons were generally bibbed and more often coloured than those of housekeepers and nurses.

A maid of all work would frequently wear an old-fashioned jacket bodice and skirt like those of the washerwoman in Pl. 6 (1772). Her caps varied but were usually mobs, either tied under the chin (old-fashioned) or with a puffed caul and frilled border. Fig. 88.

82. Maid-of-all-work, wearing a green dress, a pink neckerchief with spots, a mob cap trimmed with blue ribbon and a white apron with blue criss cross stripes, 1801.

83. Housemaids in mob caps tied under the chin. One wears a short dark dress, white apron, black stockings with holes in the heels and mules, 1835.

Thick soled shoes were usual. A vicar's wife of the time complained that the thick soles of her maid's shoes caused a "hideous clatter and wore out the carpets". (C. S. Layard, *Mrs. Lynn Linton, Her Life, Letters and Opinions*, 1901.) If, on the other hand, only shod in mules, the maid wore out her stockings (Fig. 83).

Although the overdressed maid was frowned upon, we read of "Idle sluts of maids . . . in night caps with their hair like door-mats and their gowns all open behind, and their brooms in their hands, sweeping away as make-believe, just for a minute – and then standing gossiping for at least five". (H. & A. Mayhew, *The Greatest Plague in Life*.)

Here is a list of a maid servant's requirements in 1821.

4 prs. shoos		18.	0.
2 prs. black worsted stockings		4.	0.
2 prs. white cotton ditto		5.	0.
2 gowns	1.	10.	0.
6 aprons, 4 check, 2 white		10.	6.
6 caps		10.	6.

A Bonnet, A Shawl or Cloak, Pattens, etc.
Ribbands, Handkerchiefs, Pins, Needles,
Threads, Thimbles, Scissors . . . .
Stays, stay-tape . . . etc.   2. 0. 0.
The Cook's Oracle

Boots were not usually worn and pattens (Fig. 84) were commoner in the south of England, while clogs were preferred in the north. Figs. 83, 84 and 85 show the old-fashioned quality of maid's dresses. In 1827 (Fig. 86) she was wearing a very high waist that had been the mode in 1815; in 1899 (Fig. 88) she could still wear an eighteenth century jacket bodice.

The old woman in 1874 (Fig. 87) wears a modification of the mob cap called a babet cap that had been stylish in the 1820's and 1830's. In this the head piece was gathered so as to rise up at the back.

Fig. 89, although a cartoon, is put in because, apart from the shape of the mob cap and buttoning of the cape, the clothes are typical for working women of the 1860's.

84. Maid-of-all-work in old fashioned jacket bodice, skirt pinned up all round, checked apron and pattens to keep feet dry, *c.* 1829.

85. Housemaids in old style back fastening dresses, caps and aprons, 1847.

FEMALE COOKS

All through the centuries, women cooks, like the men, nearly always wore aprons. See Pl. 45 (fourteenth century). Some kind of headgear too was essential. In the Middle Ages it might be a draped head covering, known as a coverchief or veil, but later the usual maid's cap was adopted. Their dresses were simple and the domestic neckerchief was sometimes worn, but not so frequently as by housemaids.

The following illustrations show cooks wearing aprons through the eighteenth and nineteenth centuries: Figs. 90 (eighteenth century), 91 (1790), 92(a) (b) (1816), 93 (1854), 94 (1899).

Out of doors a cook's dress would resemble that of any elderly working woman, but its style would to some extent reflect the status of her employer (Fig. 95).

The cook-maid has a somewhat different "image" from that of the cook proper. She was younger and so could double the parts of cook and parlourmaid and was more in evidence. For both reasons she tended to be more dashing in her get-up. This is well shown in Plates 47(a) (1772) and 46 (1830), also Fig. 97. These include cook-maids of three successive periods.

A last word on the women servants of the nineteenth century introduces the Step-girl of *c.* 1890.

Some of our neighbours (in lower middle class households) kept a servant, a simple *girl of about 14 in cap and apron*, and the gentility of the neighbourhood which forbade the housewife being seen cleaning her own doorstep, caused a phenomenon to appear in the form of a *step-girl*. This was a child of about 10 . . . willing to hearthstone steps, clean windows and undertake any duty that was necessary, but of such a public nature that the housewife dared not be seen doing it . . . this child provided her own *apron* (an old sack torn in half) and for a few coppers removed the fear of ostracism from the housewife . . .

Frederick Willis *A Book of London Yesterdays* 1960

86

87

86. Housemaid with high-waisted (now old fashioned) dress, blue and white striped skirt, mob cap with red ribbon, neckerchief with red spots, 1827.

87. Charwoman with skirt bunched up out of the way and sleeves rolled up. She wears a babet cap and boots. The lady wears a fashionable polonaise dress and smart hat, 1874.

88. Maid-of-all-work wearing a long skirted jacket bodice. Her dress is short. She has a bibbed apron and a small cap over untidy hair. The mistress wears a tailor-made coat and skirt costume, 1899.

THE CHAMBERMAID OF THE VATICAN.

89. Cartoon. Woman with skirt hitched up by low apron strings; pumps on the feet. A shoulder cape buttoned in front replaces the usual neckerchief and she wears a three-tiered mob cap imitating the Pope's triple crown (see text), 1869.

90. Cooks in plain dresses with bunched up overskirts, neckerchiefs, aprons and coifs. Eighteenth century.

91. Cook wearing large apron with small bib and a mob cap, *c.* 1790.

92. (*Left*) Cook in pink dress with sleeves turned up, yellow neckerchief and white cap. She is making bread, 1816. (*Right*) Cook in dark dress, yellow apron, old-fashioned mob cap and neckerchief. She is frying, 1834.

93. Smiling cook wearing apron with large bib, possibly in the absence of a neckerchief. Page boy on her left, 1854.

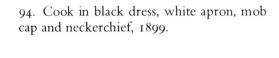

94. Cook in black dress, white apron, mob cap and neckerchief, 1899.

95. Cook in outdoor clothes, puffed out overskirt as fashionable and small bonnet. She talks to a housemaid in print dress, cap and apron, 1878.

96. Cook to eminent physician. Her small cap and high collar (with bow), instead of neckerchief, suggest extra dignity, 1882.

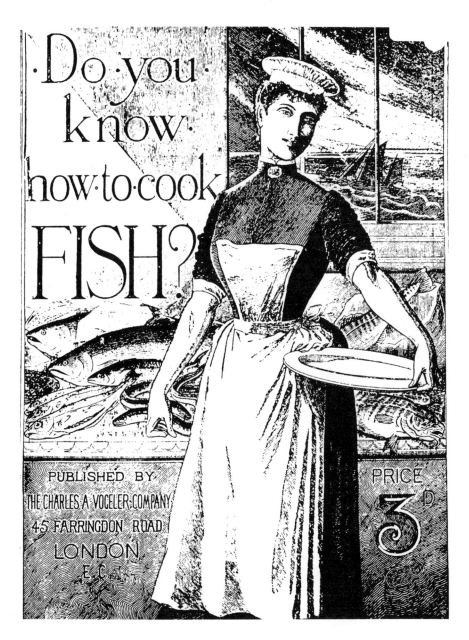

97. Young cook-maid in black dress, bibbed apron and a cap imitating the smart chef's cap of this date, known as the "Tam-o'-Shanter", 1890.

EPILOGUE ON APRONS

As the only distinctive garment worn by both sexes throughout the whole of our period, the apron has peculiar significance. First and foremost the working class apron was a symbol of menial rank.

Everyone needs protection from the cold, therefore it is not *infra dig* to wear an overcoat, but protection from dirt is another matter. It suggests undignified activity. Among servants it was demeaning to need protection from the dirt of manual work, just as in the days of private carriages it was *infra dig* to need galoshes against the mud.

We have seen the use, abuse and disuse of aprons in numerous different forms. There was everything from a piece of sacking worn for the humblest jobs, to the hygienic washable aprons needed and accepted by the cook, and there was also the tiny white apron all starch and frills whereby the parlourmaid asserted that her work was almost clean. Finally, separated by a great gulf, were all those men and women servants who, except in the pantry or my lady's bedroom, would never be seen in an apron at all.

The apron was indeed an inverted status symbol. While servants might be all below stairs, they were certainly not all below the apron. Moving among the gentry, as they did, they aspired to throw off this primitive badge of ungentlemanlike labour. Primitive it could indeed be called, for it seems to have been invented (see pl. 48) by Adam and Eve, and

> When Adam delved and Eve span
> Who was then a gentleman.[1]

---

[1] John Ball's revolutionary sermon at Blackheath in Wat Tyler's Rebellion, 1381.

148

Sources of the figures

1. Newspaper cutting, Guildhall Library, 1843.
2. W. D. F. Vincent, *British Livery Garments*, Pt. IV of *Cutters Practical Guide* [1890–5].
3a. *Life . . . of Richard Beauchamp Earl of Warwick* (1389–1439), B. M. MS., Julius E, IV art 6, f, 5v.
 b. Engraving in Francis Sandford . . . *the Solemn Interment of George Duke of Albemarle . . .* 1670.
4. Engraving from *The Noble Arte of Venerie or Hunting*, translated from the French by George Turberville, 1575.
5. Effigy, Ashwelthorpe Church, Norfolk, from C. A. Stothard, *Monumental Effigies of Great Britain*, edn. 1876.
6. "The Protestants Joy" or "An Excellent New Song on the Glorious Coronation of King William and Queen Mary" (1689), in *A Century of Ballads*, ed. J. Ashton, 1887.
7. George Paston, *Social Caricatures in the Eighteenth Century*, 1905, pl. 14 (F. Hayman pinxt. Truchy Sculpt., *c.* 1743).
8. Mrs Harriet Beecher Stowe, *Uncle Tom's Cabin*, edn. 1852.
9. *Seymour's Humorous Sketches*, eighty-six caricature etchings illus. in prose and verse by "Alfred Crowquill" (1834–6), edn. 1878.
10. B.M. MS., Tib. C VI f. 5v (detail).
11. *Aesop's Fables*, illus. by Francis Barlow *et al*, 1665.
12. "How are you off for soap?" Caricature by Elmes, pub. by Thos. Tegg, coloured impression, B.M.
13. B.M. MS., Arundel 38, f. 37 [H]occleve presenting his book (*De Regimine Principium*) to Prince Henry, shortly before his accession as Henry V, 1410–12.
14. Holbein, Queen Catherine Howard, Museum of Art, Toledo, Ohio, U.S.A.
15. Cut-out figure shown in *Gents. Magazine* (1845), New Series, vol. 24, p. 590–1.
16. From "Small Heads" by William Hogarth.

17. "Self Respect" by G. Du Maurier, *Punch*, 20 June, 1874.
18. "Servantgelism", by J. Leech, *Punch*, 1860.
19. *Illustrated London News*, 29 March, 1890, advertisment reproduced in *Victorian Advertisements*, p. 93, by L. de Vries and James Laver.
20. B.M. MS., Julius E, IV art, 6 f.10.
21. Engraving in *Noble Art of Venerie* . . . translated by G. Turberville, 1575.
22. Print, after drawing by Duncan, Mansell Collection, London.
23. C. Keene, *Punch*, 1879 (detail).
24. *Aesop's Fables*, illus. by Francis Barlow *et al*, 1665.
25. B.M. MS., Egerton, 1894.
26. Caricature by W. Heath, 1812.
27a. B.M. MS., Julius E IV art, 6 f, 7v.
   b. Ibid., f.7.
28. Randle Holme, *Academy of Armory*, 1688, Book III, ch. iii, fig. 18.
29. *Cupid and Crinoline*, pub. Rock Brothers and Payne, 20 October, 1858.
30. C. Keene, *Punch*, 1889.
31. T. H. Holding, *Uniforms of the British Army, Navy and Court*, 1894. (Section on British Liveries.)
32. J. B. Partridge, *Punch*, 1892.
33. "The Miseries of Human Life", engraved by Cruikshank, after G. M. Woodward. Coloured impression B.M. (no. 11152 in George Catalogue).
34. T. H. Holding, *Uniforms of the British Army, Navy and Court*, 1894.
35. Ibid.
36. E. T. Reed, *Punch*, 1892
37. After a photograph kindly given by Miss Brand of West Mersea.
38. T. H. Holding, *Uniforms of the British Army, Navy and Court*, 1894.
39. Ibid.
40. Albert Smith, *Sketches of London Life and Character* (illus. by Gavarin), 1859.
41. J. Couts, *Guide to Cutting*, pl. XXI (detail).
42. "The Height of Magnificence" (detail), G. du Maurier, *Punch*, 1880.
43. *Punch*, 1849.
44. MS., "Salim Horae". Facsimile in *Illustrations of a Hundred*, MSS. in the library of H. Yates Thomson, vol. 4 (1914).
45. B.M. MS., Claudius B. IV,f.31v (detail). An Anglo-Saxon MS., eleventh century.
46. B.M. MS., Cleo. C. VIII f. 18, *Psychomachia* by Aurelius Prudentius, eleventh century.
47. J. Ashton (ed.), *Humour, Wit and Satire of the Seventeenth Century*, 1883.
48. *The Miseries of Human Life* (one of a series with this title). Engraved by Cruikshank after G. M. Woodward. Coloured impression at B.M., No. 11151 in George Catalogue (detail).

49. *Chambers' Book of Days*, Vol. 1, p. 237, 1863.
50. Illustration to a 1775 edition of a satirical Restoration play first pub. 1663. Engraving after portrait of J. Moody (acting as Teague) by B. Vandergucht at the Garrick Club (detail).
51. T. H. Holding, *Uniforms of the British Army, Navy and Court*, 1894.
52. Ibid.
53. W. D. F. Vincent, *British Livery Garments* [1890–5].
54. Trinity College, Dublin MS., E.T.40.
55. *Foxe's Book of Martyrs*, edn. 1563.
56. T. H. Holding, *Uniforms of the British Army* etc., 1894.
57. Bodleian MS., Douce 88 f.501, "A Treatise on care of Horses". From reproduction in *English Rural Life in the Middle Ages*. (Bodleian Picture Book, Oxford, 1965).
58. B.M. MS., Add. 42130 (*Luttrell Psalter*).
59. *Punch*, 1866.
60. *Cupid and Crinoline*, pub. by Rock Bros. and Payne, 1858.
61. After James Gillray, "The Fashionable Mamma, or the Convenience of Modern Dress", 1796.
62. *Multiplication*, a children's book, 1816.
63. "Nurse Outwitted", *Plain Things for Little Folks*, Mary Elliot, 1823.
64. J. Leech, *Punch*, 1856.
65. "The Shy Boy" from *Baby Tales*, c. 1825., (in Children's Readers, B.M. 012806. ee. 34).
66. Newspaper cutting, Guildhall Library.
67. *Chatterbox*, No. XXXIX, 1899.
68. *Punch*, 1855.
69. *Illustrated London News*, 5 Dec. 1874, showing the christening of the first-born of the Duke and Duchess of Edinburgh.
70. *Sophia and Mary or The Sisters*, pub. by E. Wallis, 1820.
71. "The Nursery Governess", by the author of *The Week*, 1845.
72. *Punch*, 1878.
73. Frances Crompton, *The Gentle Heritage*, 1893.
74. R. Cleaver, *Punch*, 1894.
75. B.M. MS., Tib. A VII art. 5 f.90. A translation by Lydgate, made in 1426 of a poem by G. de Digulleville.
76a. G. Du Maurier, *Punch*, 1893.
  b. G. Du Maurier, *Punch*, 1894.
77. J. Leech, *Punch*, 1852.
78. H. & A. Mayhew, *The Greatest Plague in Life*, illus. by G. Cruikshank, 1847.
79. *Punch*, 1851.

L

80. B.M. MS., Tib. A VII. Art 5 f.99. A translation by Lydgate made in 1426 of a poem by G. de Digulleville.
81. Engraving in J. Heywood *The Spider and the Flie*, 1556.
82. "The Maid-of-all-work's Prayer". Engr. T. Rowlandson after G. M. Woodward, 25 July, 1801. (Pub. R. Ackermann). Coloured impression at B.M.
83. *Seymour's Humorous Sketches*. Eighty-six caricature etchings illustrated in prose and verse by "Alfred Crowquill" (1834–6), edn. 1878.
84. Cartoon: "Robertina Peelena Maid-of-all-work" by W. Heath (detail), c.1829.
85. H. & A. Mayhew, *The Greatest Plague in Life*. Illustration by G. Cruikshank, 1847.
86. W. H. Pyne, *World in Miniature*, 1827.
87. Charles Keene, *Punch*, 14 Nov. 1874.
88. *Chatterbox*, No. XXII (1899).
89. *Punch*, 1869.
90. Detail of woodcut to "A Choice Collection of Cookery Receipts", reproduced in J. Ashton *Chapbooks of the Eighteenth Century*, 1887.
91. "Mrs Fitszwarren's cross cook, beating Whittington", *Catchpenny Prints. 163 Popular Engravings from the Eighteenth Century*, originally pub. by Bowles & Carver, New York, 1970.
92. (Left and right) *Seymour's Humorous Sketches with 86 caricature etchings, illustrated in prose and verse*, by "Alfred Crowquill" (1834–6), edn. 1878.
93. *Punch*, 1854.
94. Chatterbox No. XXII, "Absence of Mind" (detail).
95. Charles Keene, *Punch*, 1878.
96. G. Du Maurier, *Punch*, 1882.
97. *The Graphic*, 6 Sept. 1890. Reproduced in *Victorian Advertisements* by L. de Vries and James Laver.

Bibliography

Publication is in London unless otherwise stated.
Abbreviations: B.M. = British Museum
　　　　　　　ed.　 = edited by
　　　　　　　edn. = edition

Adams, Samuel and Sarah, *The Complete Servant*, 1825
Aesop, Fables of, paraphrased in verse, John Ogilby, 1665. Engravings by Francis Barlow, *et al.*
Aitken, J. (ed.), *English Diaries of XVI, XVII and XVIII Centuries*, 1941.
Archenholz, J. W. von, *A Picture of England . . . 1787* (trans. 1797).
Arnold, E. *From Hall-boy to House-steward*, 1925.
Ashton, John, *Social Life in the Reign of Queen Anne*, 1882.
　(ed.), *Chap-books of the Eighteenth Century . . .* , 1882.
　(ed.), *A Century of Ballads*, 1887.
　Humour, Wit and Satire of the Seventeenth Century, 1883.

Babees Book etc., The, ed. F. J. Furnivall, E.E.T.S. O.S. 32, 1868, 1931.
Baker, Thomas, *The Fine Lady's Airs*, 1709.
Barham, Richard H., *The Ingoldsby Legends*, 1840.
Barker, Anne, *The Complete Servant Maid . . . , c.* 1770.
Bennett, Charles, *London People Sketched from Life*, 1863.
Blundell's Diary and Letter Book, 1702–28, ed. Margaret Blundell, 1952.
Bodleian Picture Books, *Portraits of the Sixteenth and early Seventeenth Centuries*, 1952. *English Illuminations of the Thirteenth and Fourteenth Centuries*, 1954. *English Rural Life in the Middle Ages*, 1965.
Book of Precedence, late Sixteenth Century. (B.M. MS. Harl. 1440). E.E.T.S. extra series VII, ed. F. C. Furnivall, 1869.
Bovill, C., *English Country Life*, 1963.
Brontë, Charlotte, *Jane Eyre*, 1847.
Busby, T. L. *Costume of the Lower Orders of London*, 1820.

153

Bibliography

Byrne, M. St. Clare, *Elizabethan Life in Town and Country*, 1961.
 The Elizabethan Home, 1949.

Carlyle, *Jane Welsh Carlyle: a new selection of her letters*, ed. Trudy Bliss, 1934.
Centlivre, Mrs. Susanna Carroll, *The Artifice* (1722) in *Dramatic Works of the celebrated Mrs Centlivre*, 1872.
Chamberlayne, Edward, *Anglicae Notitia or The Present State of England. . . .*
Chambers' *Book of Days*, 1863.
Churchyard, Thomas, *Churchyard's Chippes*, 1578.
Congreve, W., *The Way of the World*, 1700.
Cooke, Joshua, *How a Man may Choose a good wife from a bad*, in *Dodsley's Old Plays*, ed. W. C. Hazlitt, Vol. 9, 1874.
Cooke's Oracle, The, 1821.
Cooper, Charles W., *Town and County or Forty Years in Private Service with the Aristocracy*, 1937.
Costume of Yorkshire, ed. C. B. Robinson, Leeds, 1814.
Couts, J., *Practical Guide for the Tailor's Cutting Room*, 1848.
Crabbe, George, *The Library*, 1781.
Creevey's Life and Times, ed. John Gore, 1934, 1937.
Crompton, Frances, *The Gentle Heritage*, 1893.
Crosier, *The Diary of John Crosier* (1781 etc.), unpublished MS. (Essex Archaeol. Soc., Colchester).
Crowquill, see Forrester.
Cunnington, Phillis and Lucas, Catherine, *Occupational Costume in England Eleventh Century to 1914*, 1967.

Defoe, Daniel, *Moll Flanders*, 1722.
 Everybody's Business is Nobody's Business, 1725.
 Servitude, 1724, (written under the pseudonym of A. Footman).
Dekker, Thomas, *The Shoemaker's Holiday*, 1600.
Dickens, Charles, *The Pickwick Papers*, 1836–7.
D[odsley,] R., *The Footman's Friendly Advice to his Brethren of the Livery*, 1731.
Dodsley, R., *A Muse in Livery or the Footman's Miscellany*, 1732.
Dodsley's Old English Plays, ed. W. C. Hazlitt, 1874–6.

Egan, Pierce, *Tom and Jerry – Life in London*, 1869 (1st edn. 1821).
 Finish to the Adventures of Tom, Jerry and Logic, 1887, (1st edn. 1828).
Egerton Papers, The, ed. J. P. Collier (Camden Soc. 1840).
Elizabeth of York, Privy Purse Expenses of, 1503, ed. Sir N. H. Nicolas, 1830.
Ellesmere Chaucer [a Fifteenth century MS.], reproduced in facsimile, ed. Lady A. Egerton, Manchester, 1911.
Ellis, S. M. (ed.), *A Mid-Victorian Pepys*, 1863.

Bibliography

Emmison, F. G., *Tudor Secretary*, 1961.
    Tudor Food and Pastimes, 1964.
Evelyn, *The Diary of John Evelyn*, ed. Wm. Bray, 1907.
Evelyn, Mary, *Mundus Muliebris*, 1690.

Family Manual and Servants' Guide, 1856, (1st. edn. 1835).
Fanshawe, *The Memoirs of Ann Lady Fanshawe, 1600–72*, 1907.
Fairholt, F. W. ed., *Satirical Songs and Poems on Costume*, 1849.
    Costume in England 4th edn. (ed. H. A. Dillon), 1896–1909.
Farquhar, G., *The Recruiting Officers*, 1706.
    The Beaux' Stratagem, 1707.
Forrester, A. H. (pseudonym "Alfred Crowquill").
    Seymour's Humorous Sketches, 1838.
Footman, see Defoe.
Foxe, John, *Foxe's Book of Martyrs*, edn. 1563.

Galt, John, *The Ayrshire Legatees* . . . 1821.
Gentleman's Magazine, 1784.
Graham, E. Maxtone, *The Beautiful Mrs Graham and the Cathcart Circle*, 1927.
Grose, Francis ed., *Antiquarian Repertory*, Vol. I, 1807 and IV, 1809.
Grosley, Pierre Jean, *A Tour of London* . . . (1770) trans. from the French by T. Nugent, 1772.

Hamilton, Lord Frederick, *The Days before Yesterday*, 1920.
Harrison, Frederick, *Medieval Man and his Notions*, 1947.
Harrison, M. & Royston, O., *How They Lived [Vol. II] 1685–1700*, Oxford 1963.
Hassall. W. O., *How They Lived 55 B.C. – A.D. 1485*, Oxford 1962.
Haywood, Eliza, *A Present for a Servant-Maid* . . . 1743.
Hecht, J. Jean, *The Domestic Servant Class in Eighteenth Century England*, 1956.
Henderson, Wm. Augustus, *The Housekeeper's Instructor or Universal Family Cook*, 5th edn. [*c.* 1795], (1st pubd. *c.* 1793).
Hervey, *Letter Books of John Hervey, First Earl of Bristol, 1651–1750*, Vol. III. (Suffolk Green Book No. 1. 1894).
Heywood, John, *The Spider and the Flie*, 1st edn. 1556.
Hoby, *Diary of Lady Margaret Hoby, 1599–1605*, ed. D. M. Meads.
Hoccleve, T., *The Regimente of Princes* (1411), ed. F. Furnivall, 1897.
Hole, Christina, *English Home-Life 1500–1800*, 1947.
Holding, Thomas Hiram, *Uniforms of the British Army, Navy and Court*, 1894.
Holme, Randle, *Academy of Armory*, 1688.
Howard Household Books [years 1462–9], see *Manners and Household Expenses* . . .
Household Books of John Duke of Norfolk [years 1481–90], ed. J. P. Collier (Roxburghe Club 1844–5).
Hughes, Thomas, *Tom Brown's School Days*, 1856.

Jenyns, Soame, The Works of, ed. C. N. Cole 1790–1793; also article in *The World,* Vol. IV (1755).

Kalm, Pehr, *Account of his Visit to England . . . in 1748,* trans. and ed. J. Lucas, 1892.

Lanceley, William, *From Hall-Boy to House-Steward,* 1925.

Layard, C. S., *Mrs Lynn Linton, her Life, Letters and Opinions,* 1901.

Lennard, *Accounts of the Families of Lennard and Barrett 1585–1694* (Privately printed), 1908, Holly Trees Museum, Colchester.

Lestrange, *Accounts of the Lestranges of Hunstanton* (1519–78) ed. David Gurney in *Archaeologia,* Vol. 25, 411–569.

Lieven, *Private Letters of Princess Lieven to Prince Metternich 1820–6,* ed. Peter Quennell, 1948.

Lodge, E., *Illustrations of British History,* edn. 1838.

Lovell, George, *Look before you leap,* c. 1846.

Lovell, Sir Thomas, Household Accounts, in *Middleton MSS.* (Royal Hist. MSS. Commission, 1905).

Machyn, *The Diary of Henry Machyn, Citizen & Merchant Taylor of London from A.D. 1550–1563,* ed. John G. Nichols (Camden Soc.) 1848.

Manners and Household Expenses in the Thirteenth and Fifteenth Centuries, Roxburghe Club, 1841.

Markham, Gervase, *The English Hus-wife* (1615) in *"Country Contentments",* Book II; See also I.M.

I.M. [attrib. Gervase Markham], *A Health to the Gentlemanly Profession of Serving-Men* [1598]. ed. A. V. Judges, 1931.

Marshall, Dorothy, *The English Domestic Servant in History,* 1949.

Marshe, Thomas, see Churchyard, Thomas.

Massinger, Philip, *A New Way to Pay Old Debts* (1630), edn. 1897.

Mayhew, H. & A., *The Greatest Plague in Life,* 1847.

Meadows, Joseph K., *Heads of the People . . .* Drawn by Kenny Meadows, 1841.

Medieval English Verse, trans. and ed. Brian Stone (Penguin Classics, 1964).

Middleton MSS., see Lovel, Sir Thomas.

Middleton, Thomas, *A Mad World My Masters* (1608).

Misson, Henri, *M. Misson's Memoirs and Observations in his Travels over England,* trans. John Ozell, 1719.

Montagu, *Elizabeth Montagu the Queen of the Blue Stockings,* ed. E. Climenson, 1906.

Morton, Thomas, *The Way to get Married,* 1796.

Moritz, *Travels of Carl Philip Moritz in England in 1782,* English trans. of 1795 ed. P. E. Matheson, 1924.

Myers, A. R. (ed.), *The Black Book and Ordinance of 1478,* Manchester University Press, 1958.

Bibliography

Newton, Lady, *Lyme Letters 1660–1760*, 1925.

Nichols, John (ed.), *Progresses and Public Processions . . . of Queen Elizabeth*, edn. 1823.

North, Extracts from the Household Books of Lord North (1575–6) *Archaeologia*, Vol. 19, pp. 283–301.

O'Keeffe, J., *Tony Lumpkin in Town*, 1780.

Overbury, Sir Thomas. *The Overburian Characters . . .* (1614), ed. W. J. Payler, Oxford, 1936.

Paston Letters, (1422–73), with notes by John Fenn, ed. A. Ramsay, 1840.

Paston, George, *Social Caricatures in the Eighteenth Century*, 1905.

Peacham, H., *The Worth of a Penny*, 1641.

Pennant, Thomas, *An Account of London*, 1790.

Pepys, Samuel, *Diary 1659–69*, ed. Henry B. Wheatley, 1926.

Percival, Viscount, *Diary*, 1729.

Purefoy Letters, 1735–53, ed. G. Eland, 1931.

Pyne, W. H., *The World in Miniature*, 1827.

Richard II, *Historia Vitae et Regni Ricardi Secundi* (ascribed to a monk of Evesham), ed. Thomas Hearne, 1729.

Roche, Sophie von la, *Sophie in London, 1786, being the Diary of Sophie v. la Roche*, trans. and ed. Clare Williams, 1933.

Rochefoucauld, Francois de la, *A Frenchman in England, 1784*, trans. S. C. Roberts, Cambridge, 1933.

Roxburghe Ballads, ed. W. Chappell. 1869.

Rutland, *MSS. of the Duke of Rutland* (Royal Hist. MSS. Commission) 1905.

Shakespeare, Wm., Plays.

Scott Thomson, Gladys, *The Russells of Bloomsbury, 1669–1771*. 1940.

Sheridan, *Betsy Sheridan's Journal*, ed. William Lefanu, 1960.

Sibbald, *The Memoirs of Susan Sibbald (1783–1812)*, ed. Francis Paget Hett, 1926.

Silliman, Benjamin, the elder, *A Journal of Travels . . . in the years 1805–6*. 3rd edn. New Haven 1820.

Smith, Albert (ed.), *Sketches of London Life and Character*, 1859.

Smollett, Tobias G., *Humphrey Clinker*, 1771.

Smyth, James, *Scarromides*, 1692.

Spenser, Edmund, *The Faerie Queen*, 1590.

Stapleton, *Household Books of Sir Miles Stapleton, 1661* in *The Ancestor*, Vol. 3.

Stow, John, *A Survey of London*, ed. C. L. Kingsford, Oxford, 1952 (1st edn. 1598).

Stowe, Harriet Beacher, *Uncle Tom's Cabin*, 1852.

Stuart, Dorothy M., *The English Abigail*, 1946.

Bibliography

Stubbes, Philip, *The Anatomie of Abuses* (1583), ed. F. C. Furnivall, 1878–82.
Surtees, R. S., novels.
Swift, Jonathan, *Directions to Servants in General and in particular to . . .* (written before 1738).

Taine, H., *Notes on England*, trans. with intro. by W. F. Rae, 1872.
Taylor, Tom, *Still Waters Run Deep*, 1855.
Thackeray, W. M., novels.
Thomson, Gladys Scott, *The Russells in Bloomsbury*, 1660–1771, 1940.
Townley, Rev. James, *High Life Below Stairs*, 1759.
Trollope, Frances, *The Life and Adventures of Michael Armstrong the Factory Boy*, edn. 1840.
Trusler, John, *Trusler's Domestic Management*, edn. Bath, 1819.
Turbervile, G. (trans.), *Noble Arte of Venerie or Hunting* [1575–6].

Udall, Nicholas, *Ralph Roister Doister*, 1540.

Vincent, W. D. F., *British Livery Garments . . .* , being Part IV of The Cutter's Practical Guide . . . [1890–5].
Vries, Leonard de, *Victorian Advertisements*, text by James Laver, 1968.

Williams, Ernest N., *Life in Georgian England . . .* , 1962.
Willis, Frederick, *Book of London Yesterdays*, 1960.
Wilson, Angus, *The World of Charles Dickens*, 1970.
Wilson, E., *History of the Glove Trade*, 1834.
Woodforde, *The Diary of a Country Parson, The Rev. James Woodforde* (1758–1802), ed. John Beresford, 1924–31 (5 vols.).
Wright, Thomas, *A History of Domestic Manners and Sentiments in England during the Middle Ages*, 1862.
Wolley, Hannah, *The Complete Serving Maid*, 1685 (1st edn. 1677).
     The Gentlewoman's Companion or a Guide to the Female Sex, 1675.
Yorkshire, *Rural Economy in Yorkshire in 1641*, ed. C. B. Robinson, 1857.

PERIODICALS

Ancestor, Vols. 2 and 4.
Archaeologia IX, XXV.
Illustrated London News, Vol. 96.
Ipswich Journal, 1765.
London Chronicle, 1791.
London Evening Post, 1738.
Mercurius Politicus, 1658.
Notes and Queries, Series V, Vol. V.

Bibliography

Punch, Vols. 1853, 1860, 1866, 1873, 1883.
The Sartor or British Journal of Cutting, Clothing and Fashion, Vol. III, Nov. 1871.
Spectator, No. 299, 1712.
Sussex Archaeological Collections, Vol. III.
Sylvia's Home Journal, 1879.
Tailor and Cutter, 1897.
Tatler, No. 132, 1709.
The Times, 1795.
Weekly Journal, 1726.
West End Gazette of Fashion, 1865.
The World, Vol. IV, 1755.

ILLUMINATED MANUSCRIPTS

A glossed Psalter, B.M. MS. Tib. C.VI (11th Century).
An Anglo-Saxon Pentateuch, B.M. MS. Claudius B.IV (Eleventh Century).
    Aurelius Prudentius, *Psychomachia* (copy made in England), B.M. MS.
    Cleo C VIII (Eleventh Century).
Trinity College Dublin MS. E. I 40 (Thirteenth Century).
Decretals of Pope Gregory IX, B.M. MS. Roy. 10 E.IV (early Fourteenth
    Century).
Queen Mary's Psalter, B.M. MS. Roy. 2 B.VII (*c.* 1320).
"*The Trinity Apocalypse*", Trinity College Cambridge MS. R. 16.2 (1325–50).
    Facsimile by P. Brieqer, 1967.

Luttrell Psalter, B.M. MS. Add. 42130 (*c.* 1340).
De Regimine Principum, B.M. MS. Arundel 38 (1410–12).
Lydgate's translation in 1426, of a poem by G. de Digulleville. B.M. MS.
    Tib. A. VII (Fifteenth Century).
Froissart's Chronicle. B.M. MS. Harl. 4380 (late Fifteenth Century).
Pageant of the Earl of Warwick, B.M. MS. Julius E.IV art. 6 (1485–90).
Funeral of Queen Elizabeth, B.M. MS. Add. 35324 ff. 27–37 (early Seventeenth
    Century).

Index

DIARIES, HOUSEHOLD
ACCOUNTS, ETC., QUOTED: